ANOREXIA NERVOSA:
LET ME BE

Let Me Be

Anorexia Nervosa: Let Me Be

A. H. Crisp
St George's Hospital Medical School
London

Routledge
Taylor & Francis Group

LONDON AND NEW YORK

**This is a reprint of a title
originally published in
1980 by Academic Press**

First published by
Lawrence Erlbaum Associates Ltd., Publishers
10 Industrial Avenue
Mahwah, New Jersey 07430

Transferred to Digital Printing 2009 by Routledge
27 Church Road, Hove, East Sussex, BN3 2FA
270 Madison Ave, New York NY 10016

Routledge is an imprint of the Taylor & Francis Group; an informa business.

British Library Cataloguing in Publication Data

A catalogue record for this book is available from the British Library

   ISBN 978-0-86377-383-9 (pbk)

Cover by The Design Revolution

Publisher's Note
The publisher has gone to great lengths to ensure the quality of this reprint
but points out that some imperfections in the original may be apparent.

Preface

Anorexia nervosa, a distorted biological solution to an existential problem for an adolescent and her (or occasionally his) family, is a crippling condition. Experienced as adaptive in the face of an otherwise imminent crisis, it results, through its massive and abortive effect on physical, psychological and social development, in increasingly destructive isolation for the individual as the years go by. Although it is the most primitive of avoidance responses to the immediate problems of adolescence, it does not always reflect the absence of actual or potential and more effective life-sustaining resources within the individual and family. Indeed, in my view many people with anorexia nervosa can be helped to a better adjustment to and engagement with adult biological and social life. This book has been written in an attempt to share these views, in the hope that they will sometimes be useful to people with the condition and their families as well as to would-be helpers.

Preface to 1995 Reprint

I am delighted that Lawrence Erlbaum Associates have adopted this book and are immediately reprinting it. It naturally pleases me that health care professionals, sufferers and their families continue to want to read it. During the last 15 years we have demonstrated in a systematic way that treatment based on the model outlined in this book works. Not everyone can be helped to recover but those who cannot often show a great capacity to find some fulfilment despite the persistent illness. Moreover, the number of deaths from the condition at 20-25 year follow-up is much less than expected. All these research findings are published in papers which are amongst those listed at the end of the book.

This reprint coincides with my required retirement from the NHS in the UK, a service I have been proud to work in for the past 40 years. It was in 1960 that I first established the model and basis of this treatment programme and since then it has developed with the help of very many people such as those acknowledged overleaf.

February 1995   Arthur Crisp

Acknowledgements 1979

During the past 20 years I have worked clinically in this field with many people. They include psychiatrists, social workers, nurses and many anorectics. In particular I learned a great deal from Eugene Wolf at the Middlesex Hospital, London, who first introduced me to some of the skills of family therapy; also more recently Ted Stonehill, Britta Harding, Ross Kalucy and many others at St George's Hospital, London, with whom I have had the privilege of sharing some such insights into the nature of anorexia nervosa as I believe there to be. I am deeply grateful to have had the good fortune to work with so many such people.

This short book has been inordinately long in the making because I have had to come back to it as time allowed since 1975. It would not have materialized at all without the professional skills of Heather Humphrey who has typed and retyped the manuscript, unobtrusively reconstituting the split infinitives and gently advising against my more tortuous sentences.

I also express my gratitude to Alan Jones, who has been responsible for the diagrams, to Anne Hart, who has recently been closely involved in our projective art therapy, of which the paintings and drawings in this book are examples, and to Susan Letham who with me undertook the dietary surveys depicted in Figures 1-8. Finally, I would also like to thank all the patients who have so honestly contributed the material on which this book is based, especially those whose drawings, paintings and descriptions of experiences have been specifically included.

Additional Acknowledgements 1995

Over the last 16 years many other colleagues have made major contributions to my own thinking and to the further development of the service. I have been most fortunate in having a series of outstanding clinical lecturers to work with me, all of whom share the necessary understanding and skills both as clinicians and scientists. Sequentially they include Hubert Lacey, Charnie Chen, Tom Burns, George Hsu, Alison Hall, Kingsley Norton, Simon Gowers, Neil Joughin and Lisa McClelland. Other colleagues have also played an important part; they include Bob Palmer, David Ben-Tovim, Denise Yeldham, Barbara Rooney (medical), Carol Bowyer (nutritionist), Aurelie Freeman and Nicola McCarry (social workers), Chris Halek, Stephanie Jurczak, Lea Jordan, Richard Edgeworth, and Chris Prestwood (nursing), Liz Mitchell, Gill Levett, Philip Tata and Marina Perris (psychology), Shena Duncan, Rachel Eastman, Catherine Jo (occupational therapy), Ashok Bhat, Dette Lynch, Richard Atkinson (biostatisticians), and many others — the list could be almost endless. To all the unnamed, the named and above all the patients, I reaffirm my gratitude.

Contents

To the team, the "patients" and those who care.

SECTION I
Anorexia Nervosa as an Illness

1
Introduction

The term "anorexia nervosa", although hallowed by time and usage and by the fine clinical descriptions of the underlying disorder that accompanied its introduction, is in certain ways an unfortunate one to apply to the condition that is the subject of this book.

The term implies that the disorder is rooted in a nervous loss of appetite. Loss of appetite in its turn infers a loss of interest in, desire for, orientation towards food. By way of contrast, the person with anorexia nervosa usually displays an excess of these characteristics. What further characterizes her (I am often going to use the female pronoun in a generic sense since the majority of people with the condition are female, but it should not be forgotten that about one in ten individuals with it is male), is the fact that she does not follow up this excessive interest and impulse by eating food, or if she does, she will immediately need to contrive its elimination from her system, before it becomes part of her body and herself. This resistance to eating or to the retention of ingested food is the obvious hallmark of the condition. It provides clues to the underlying experiential needs of the individual and it contrasts with what most doctors would agree on as a classical state of anorexia—namely a simple loss of appetite—which is a feature of many other medical conditions. Thus the latter is characteristic of states of severe disturbance of mood, for instance anxiety and depression and their related psychiatric syndromes, and also of many debilitating physical illnesses.

English language references to what is clearly anorexia nervosa can be traced back to medical writings of the seventeenth century and, 100 years ago, the disorder was described in great clinical detail by several physicians of the time. It says a great deal for the perspicacity of those doctors that they recognized it as a fundamentally distinct entity amongst the welter of emaciating diseases of young people then present. For, as I shall explain later, it is not a state which is readily revealed. The person with it does not as a rule see herself as afflicted—on the contrary she

3

resists change and continually strives to conceal the true state of affairs. Because of this evident quality of blandness in and acceptance of the condition by the person with it, especially when thrust into the role of "patient", the physicians of the last century concluded that psychological factors were possibly at its roots. Indeed, in France, where it was well-recognized at the time, there were some who concluded that it showed many of the features of hysteria—a state very much in the public eye because of the advent of the technique of hypnosis to which people with such disorders sometimes responded dramatically. In such ways the clinical medical discipline of psychiatry became involved in attempting to help some people with the condition. Psychiatry, as a medical discipline mainly concerned with mental illness, wherein it has been assumed that both social and psychological factors as well as bodily factors were contributing to the disorder in question, and where the disorders themselves were often manifest in terms of the patients' reported experience of their personal distress, with little in the way of physical signs being present, has often been almost overly concerned to categorize the disorders confronting it. Psychiatrists' attempts to do just this to anorexia nervosa have a familiar ring to them. Over the past century, anorexia nervosa has been classified as every kind of neurosis or else insanity. Diagnosis is regarded as crucial in medicine, and this essential aim stems from the need to classify each new disorder encountered in terms of known categories. Only then can the outlook for the disease process become established and suitable treatments be instituted. The first steps in recognizing disease entities are usually those of identifying relevant clusters of symptoms and signs. These must be found to characterize the entity and to separate it off in their terms from other symptoms and signs reflecting other entities, with which there is not much overlap. A later stage is often the identification of a discrete pathological process within the body which is generating the clinical features. Later still one hopes to understand its chemistry. In psychiatry we are very much at the stage of recognizing "disease" entities in terms of clinical phenomena—symptoms and signs. Some would argue that with psychiatric disorders it is not possible to impose this medical model of disease. Others would claim that such disorders do have some common biological and behavioural qualities which distinguish them from each other. It is upon this matrix of syndromes within psychiatry, with emphasis upon underlying neuropathology, that attempts have been made to superimpose the state of anorexia nervosa. As subsequent chapters will reveal, I believe this to have been a misdirected endeavour.

I see anorexia nervosa more as a psychologically adaptive stance operating within biological mechanisms. It is the particular state of starvation unique to the condition that meets the psychosocial needs of the person concerned. Thus, anorexia nervosa is a disorder of adolescents, very much more common in the female than the male and it is the thrust of puberty that has introduced body weight and shape as a new, meaningful and threatening experience for those concerned. The significance of food in the condition has to do with its relationship to body weight and shape, and not directly to its symbolic relationship to the mother.

On the whole, I also consider it useful to view anorexia nervosa as an illness, as it is possible to detect, often at a glance, the major physical disability and unusual behaviour which characterize the condition, as does, even more specifically, the individual's underlying and often hidden, destructive though dominating psychosocial needs. The psychobiological mechanism invoked by these latter needs which generates the physical disability and abnormal behaviour also seems to be highly specific to the condition. It can result in death, and otherwise often chronically damages normal biological (e.g. the capacity to have children) and social (e.g. the capacity to work and to love) development and health. Moreover, attempted therapeutic medical and psychosocial intervention can probably influence its course. The fact that the individual with the condition often does not see herself as ill, places anorexia nervosa in the same category as many other disorders with a seemingly evident medical component, such as alcoholism, obesity, schizophrenia, etc. As such it will always be important to society to protect the rights of the person with anorexia nervosa; and for non-medical specialists such as nurses, psychologists and sociologists to recognize that they may have a role in trying to help people afflicted with the condition who are attempting to struggle free from it. In this book the author, a psychiatrist, will in the first instance endeavour to examine anorexia nervosa within an "illness" framework. However, before proceeding further with the theme of anorexia nervosa itself it will be worthwhile to examine briefly some of the ways in which other cultures and other societies in history have dealt with such matters as puberty and adolescence, and ways in which feasting, fasting and the stance of ascetism have become incorporated into their lifestyles. The sources of such information range from Fraser's Golden Bough to the writings of Mead and Malinowski.

As we shall see, despite the fact that anorexia nervosa is predominantly a disorder of affluent and westernized societies, anthropological findings show us that food, eating and sexual attitudes and behaviour are closely related in many cultures remote from our own. However, there is very little concern with body weight and shape as a possible intervening variable. In primitive and subsistence-level cultures, fatness seems to be less explicitly associated with sexuality in the female (except perhaps in some of the fertility symbols and deities of Stone Age and related cultures where the goddesses are portrayed as heavy-thighed and obese) than with health and wealth.

Anthropological studies have been largely of American, African and Mediterranean cultures, and Polynesian and Aboriginal cultures in the islands of the South Pacific. Although Mead briefly describes the impact of western Christian missionaries on such cultures, the intrinsic pre-Christian behaviour of these groups is the essence of the anthropologist's contribution. The striking thing is the universality of certain themes, and in contrast the rich diversity of specific ritual and custom that they generate.

Puberty

In many tribal cultures in the American sub-continent, Africa and Asia, the menarche was taken as the specific indicant of female puberty. It led to both immediate ritual and also the establishment of new customs and sometimes also taboos for the individual concerned thereafter. The first menstrual flow was often regarded by men in the tribe as potentially very damaging to themselves, should such a girl look upon them. The concept that the girl was infectious often existed and, in particular, that she might poison the earth with her menstrual blood, rendering it infertile or otherwise poisonous to their food supply. Equally she might be liable to fertilization by the sun at this time. In some cultures girls were wrapped up and slung in hammocks away from the public eye, suspended between earth and sky. Often food was denied them or they would not eat, and sometimes became emaciated. Only when menstrual flow had definitely ceased would they be freed.

Among South Sea islanders, girls were often shut away in huts during the first menstrual flow and only allowed to eat certain and selected foods such as fish. Customs such as throwing coconuts into the sea and bathing the girl in coconut milk have been described. In such cultures the period of abstinence from food is sometimes followed by a series of feasts, for instance with rice as a basis. Such foods lend themselves to interpretation as fertility and sexual symbols. Puberty rites are often followed by the imposition on the new adolescent of taboos and customs. She may be required to leave the family home, seemingly to avoid incest and also envy by the mother. Sometimes she remains largely isolated and in limbo for a considerable period of time, or else she may mingle only with her own female peer group and remain a virgin. In societies with such rigid rules, transgression of them can be followed by punitive measures directed not only at the girl but also at the extended family. In other tribal cultures sexual relationships with young men are encouraged at this stage.

With no single incident like the menarche to focus on as the pivotal point of sexual maturation, the achievement of male adulthood tended in many tribal cultures to be marked by age-related ceremonies, often staggered over quite a wide age-range, say 12 to 16 years. Progressive separation from his family and home was often demanded of the boy, coupled with integration into his male peer group, mastery of weapons, trials of strength, courage and sometimes sexual prowess. In some tribes a major ritual involved a symbolic killing of the boy, sometimes associated with his disappearance from the tribe for a while, followed by his re-emergence as a mature male.

It may be concluded then, that in many tribal societies, puberty is recognized as a major maturational process requiring recognition by the tribe, the family and the individual concerned. It is associated with immediate rituals often involving isolation, abstinence from eating in the female, and by the requirement that the adolescent conduct herself or himself in ways consonant with the tribe's customs concerning adolescence. If such rules are flouted then punishment or banishment may follow.

Fasting and Feasting

The practice of fasting is an almost universal feature of human societies. It is sometimes rooted in magical beliefs and otherwise has an explicit symbolic meaning within the culture. In its more sustained form it blends into a type of ascetism and, in this latter context in particular, there is often an explicit and implicit awareness that the process is associated with the control and stifling of other bodily desires.

Throughout history, fasting has been recognized in some cultures as a weapon of personal or public protest. Within Celtic tribes a person or group would "fast against" someone or some other tribe or group who had been unjust to them. The concept of fasting as an act of revenge is found in parts of the New Testament. The hunger strike has become a feature of modern political life, intended to rouse popular support through martyrdom and to manipulate opponents in the process. Fasting has sometimes been undertaken under public scrutiny, ostensibly for competitive purposes and for personal gain. Finally, some Indian and Polynesian tribes having presumably sensed the link between the potential fertility of their newly sewn crops and their sexuality used to fast and remain celibate during the spring period. Others, in contrast, would become excessively sexually active at this time, believing that this would enhance growth of the seed.

Commonest by far of all the uses of voluntary fasting are those associated with self-denial and with related religious practices. Whilst the extremes of asceticism are more characteristic of those philosophies and religions which are based in the dualistic notion of mind and body as separate entities, fasting as a more episodic and symbolic exercise of self-denial has characterized societies rooted in both monistic and dualistic thinking.

In the more primitive societies, rich with magical belief and a spectrum of related good and evil influences and deities operating outside themselves and on the fringe of their tribe, fasting was often adopted as an explicit self-punishment in an attempt to placate the wrath of either the tribal leaders or the tribal gods. In ancient Indian and Mediterranean cultures fasting, sometimes together with other sacrifices, was again usually undertaken as an act of penance or placation. In Hinduism, restricted eating and other austerities characterize the caste system and are also linked to pilgrimages. Permanent dietary restrictions and periods of fasting related to atonement are features of Judaism. Mohammedans fast strenuously, sometimes to the point of exhaustion, during Ramadān, and are also required to fast as a punishment for certain offences. Even within the monistic philosophies of Buddhism and Taoism, fasting is a feature of their more strict adherents, again associated with self-denial and penance. Imposed fasting, as distinct from loss of appetite, also characterizes grief and mourning in many societies.

Finally, fasting should be seen in contrast to feasting and it is in this link that the association with sexuality becomes more explicit. In tribal cultures fasting is often required of the engaged or would-be married couple. In contrast the marriage itself is celebrated by extended feasting and with many ceremonies involving food, for instance the scattering of rice over the couple. Carnivals (literally *farewell to flesh*) typically precede or follow a period of fasting. The Christian religion has a richer and more widespread tradition of fasting practices than any other, and its related cultures sometimes also show this link between fasting and feasting. For instance, Easter, a time of birth and rebirth, is preceded by the abstinence of Lent, and is a time of eating and festivity through the incorporation of pre-Christian pagan practices into the celebration—for example the consumption of Easter eggs.

Fasting associated with Christianity provides us with a wealth of cultural background information relevant to our own present day society and perhaps therefore the more related to anorexia nervosa, which is so much a disorder related to this society.

Jesus Christ taught by example. He fasted at times, sometimes for many days and, famously, whilst in the wilderness. Subsequently fasting became a feature of the doctrine and custom of the Church, related specifically to festivals and to events such as baptism and holy communion, and to certain days of the week. In the next few centuries, at a time of widespread persecution of Christians, and before the emergence of the early monasteries which allowed a different kind of self-denial and retreat, the custom was widespread as was the more extreme ascetic stance rooted in personal abstinence from food and sexual activity.

Such practices survived the reformation of the Church in England although later they often took a more moderate form. Rigorous fasting later re-emerged as a feature of many Puritan and evangelical sects. The practice of fasting survives to this day, especially during Lent. Roman Catholic Holy Communion, involving the concept of transubstantiation— the process whereby bread, blessed and eaten, is converted into divine substance—the flesh of God, officially requires that fasting has occurred beforehand. This same doctrine of transubstantiation itself was familiar to the Aryans of ancient India before the rise of Christianity and to early Central American Indian civilizations.

Finally, feasting, already described in relation to fasting and clearly thereby related to celebrations of either a secular or holy kind, is also often a feature of societies wherein it is unrelated to a phase of fasting and purification. South Sea islanders in the past seem to have been very much like us in that births, marriages and anniversaries were often ritualistically marked by feasting. Feasting was also a feature of the cementing of good relationships between families and tribes and of the releasing of adolescents from their taboos and other restrictions concerning sexual relationships.

Ascetism

Ascetism involves the seeking of an ideal goal through training. Popular usage of the word restricts it to goals that are seen as virtuous. The process of attaining such goals usually involves rigorous self-control, both physical and mental.

Although such practices have been widespread amongst certain groups in nearly all cultures in recorded history they have probably been most common amongst cultures with an explicit dualistic philosophy of mind and body. Within such dualism the body has always seemed to be potentially corrupting of the mind and self-control and self-punishment have frequently been directed at it in the first instance. Thus men have sometimes found that social ascetical practices such as monastic isolation, a totally solitary life, silence and prayer, have facilitated pious and sometimes mystical thought, but usually an element of corresponding physical rigour has also been built in. This might involve hard physical work, limited time spent in bed and sometimes the specific self-imposition of discomfort or pain or mutilation. More often it has also involved, often fundamentally so, frugal eating and sexual abstinence. The evil body and passions are not to be pandered to, but instead stifled. The early ascetics are often popularly portrayed as scrawny, restless people. In Indian society ascetism has been more associated with attempts to transcend the cycle of growth and decay and instead achieve union with the creative and pervasive life forces themselves—a mystical aim. In Christian society the emphasis has been more on atonement for sins and placation of God.

It will be argued that these two forces, of reunion on the one hand and purification, placation and conformity on the other, sought and sometimes achieved through the abstinent and self-denying physical ascetic stance, are important mechanisms in anorexia nervosa, though usually mobilized directly in respect of immediate family forces rather than their extensions and projections into wider society and philosophies.

2
Immediate Clinical Features of the Condition: Physical, Behavioural, Experiential

The doctor usually encounters anorexia nervosa of recent onset when the individual concerned is brought to him by worried parents or other people. More rarely, the chronically ill anorectic consults a doctor on her own, either seeking help for some physical complication of her hidden condition but without wishing for her fundamental adjustment to be revealed or changed, or even seeking to involve the unenlightened doctor in adopting a course of action which will actually strengthen her own capacity to control low body weight. More rarely still the anorectic will spontaneously consult a doctor seeking help to free herself from her condition.

Physical Features

The immediate and striking clinical feature is usually emaciation. The anorectic is not just a thinnish person, small boned but fully formed; she is skeletal in appearance and with a marked absence of subcutaneous fat. She may weigh as little as four to five stones (56-70 lbs; 25-32 kgs), but the usual person presenting in the clinic weighs around 5½ to 6½ stones (77-91 lbs; 35-41 kgs). She may wear clothes of a kind which effectively mask much of her bodily appearance but her face is likely to look gaunt, though it may rarely be puffy if she has recently overeaten. Swelling of the ankles if present is a more chronic feature and is almost always an indicator of severe starvation associated with low protein levels and severe electrolyte disturbance in the tissues. These latter disturbances are features of current, chronic and often secretive vomiting and/or excessive purging and diuretic dependence. The anorectic's extremities are usually cold and often red or blue in colour. Chilblains are not uncommon.

Usually it is the individual's emaciated state and inability to eat that has precipitated the consultation. Either those involved with her have reached saturation point in terms of their exasperation and helplessness or else there has been some deterioration in the individual's physical state causing alarm to others, e.g. further weight loss or a revealed spate of vomiting. Occasionally the individual presents as a medical emergency. She may have become so weak that she can no longer stand; she may have begun to faint frequently. Occasionally the condition can present with symptomatic epilepsy or because the individual has begun to produce large quantities of urine, with gastro-intestinal stasis, acute dilatation of the stomach or some other acute functional and life-threatening disturbance that requires rapid appraisal of the underlying abnormal metabolic state.

Further examination of the physical state will reveal that the individual has not been having her monthly menstrual periods. Exceptions to this presentation may arise if (i) she is having bleeds associated with periodic withdrawal of the "Pill", (ii) if she is in a posture of low weight control associated with extreme bingeing and vomiting (this state is associated even at quite low weights with a relatively high basal metabolic rate and associated preservation of menstrual function), or (iii) inaccurate reporting due either to lack of knowledge of normal menstrual function or denial or concealment of the real situation.

Often there is a fine downy hair called lanugo hair but indistinguishable from villous hair over the body, especially over the back and face. The pulse rate usually is slow, in the range 40-60 beats per minute, unless the individual has recently eaten. (Once again, if she has recently binged the pulse may be racing.) Consonant with her general hypometabolic state her blood pressure will be low by normal standards, say 90/60 mm of mercury. These cardiovascular features, along with the cold hands and feet and generally low body temperature, reflect the body's conservation mechanisms to the challenge of starvation and are not necessarily indications of acute physiological decompensation and imminent medical crisis.

Aspects of Behaviour

At this first encounter, a not infrequent feature of the person with the condition is that she prefers to stand rather than sit when waiting. It is a sad sight to see such a helpless silent family group with the emaciated daughter thus slightly detached and on one side—it gives a first important impression of time stood still.

This frequently present barrier is invariably brought into the first few minutes of the consultation and indeed presents the first of many major challenges to any would-be therapist. Failure to penetrate it will be associated with a persistence of denial of difficulties and sullen or desperate restatements that others have misjudged the situation. Meanwhile, the preoccupations of others will be related to concern over her eating and body weight. No concept of her having sacrificed anything for the family exists.

Only when one has really got to know an anorectic patient can such a position begin to be seen as having some other basis. Then, through the still reluctant account of the anorectic herself or, more likely, through the accounts of parents, friends and any other observers of her previous behaviour, a history of other behaviour also linked to the condition begins to be revealed. The evolution of this behaviour will be discussed in Chapter 3. For the present the spectrum of such behaviour will be described.

Adjectives such as furtive, secretive, hostile, stubborn, withdrawn, sad, are commonly used to describe the anorectic manner, by those around her. Families come to realize that any pressure on their daughter to eat is likely to lead to an outburst of rage and tears. She has come to control the situation to such an extent that everyone else feels that they must deal very carefully indeed with her. The anorectic's stance has this in common with that of the hysteric; that her position is such a last ditch stand, her only and primitive resource, and potentially so unstable that she cannot allow any intrusion by others into her adjustment. Indeed, she is often seen by them as occupying an exclusive, tyrannical position. Occasionally, as an aspect of this defensive mechanism, the anorectic will present a bright and breezy or bland manner to the outside world. More often however, especially if caught unawares, she looks, as has previously been said, sad and miserable, or else breathlessly and totally preoccupied with herself.

Activity

The majority of anorectics are very restless—for instance they walk or bicycle or stand whenever possible. They sleep less than others and may be particularly active early in the mornings.

Often they appear to others to be preoccupied with calorie counting and with food preparation. They may have taken over the family cooking arrangements although they will, of course, rarely eat the food themselves. Other members of the family may begin to gain weight! Ritualistic behaviour—seemingly irrelevant repetitive actions—may come to surround such preparation, especially those small quantities of non-carbohydrate food that the abstaining anorectic prepares for herself. She may begin to eat alone, in her bedroom, or at times other than those of family mealtimes. She may not allow others to see her eat. Hoarding food may become a dominant feature, for instance tins of food or else food prepared for eating but instead hidden away, but not discarded. Equally, food thought by others to have been eaten by the anorectic is instead thrown away.

The anorectic's central though commonly denied concern is that she avoid gaining weight. Opposition to eating is rooted and only rooted in this need. Not eating for longer than a few hours at a time is a miserable affair for most of us and the anorectic, perhaps more than most of us, is potentially someone who could get pleasure from eating. If, after months of abstinence and isolation, she discovers that she can eat and yet, by subsequent vomiting, not gain weight, then she may settle for this. Whereas before she would, in her attempt to slim, have excluded most or all recognizable carbohydrate from her diet, now she may eat indiscriminately, albeit often still secretly and not infrequently mainly at night. Those around the anorectic may be aware of such behaviour but, even when it is as frequent as several times a day, they may remain unaware of the vomiting. Such families become amazed that their daughter eats so much yet does not gain weight—the first law of thermo-dynamics appears to have been successfully challenged. A clue for them, as for the doctor when his patient disappears to the toilet immediately after her interview with him, is that after each meal the anorectic regularly and instantly disappears for some while, usually to the toilet or bathroom. Most anorectics are very reluctant to eat in public and avoid restaurants at any price—a restaurant creates meal conditions wherein they may lose control over what they eat and retain.

Consonant with the underlying needs of their stance, anorectics, chronologically young or old, often train and work in such fields as dancing (particularly the ballet with its special rigours), fashion, nutrition, and the hotel and restaurant trade.

Experiential

Probably in no other morbid condition is the outsider more effectively and so frequently denied access to an appreciation of the relationship between behaviour and manner on the one hand and inner experience on the other than is the case with the anorectic.

The anorectic's area of private distress, her capacity to keep secret her inner fears and preoccupations, stems partly from her sense of the precariousness of her defensive stance and her inability to risk exposure. Also, much of the past tumultuous experience which immediately preceded her illness is no longer relevant—so extreme is her avoidance posture. Other people are usually kept at bay by statements such as "I am eating normally" or "I am eating enough" or "I've just lost my appetite and interest in food". Consonant with this is the anorectic's report to others that she estimates herself as being fatter than she is. This is often a very complex statement. It embodies a characteristic experience of most adolescent females to consider themselves fat and to overestimate the latter's degree in terms of their shape and size in association with a sense of distaste or disgust (two words already showing the link between shape, fatness and eating). The fact that the majority of such adolescent girls are not obese in a medical sense invites the profound question: "What is the fatness that they dislike so much and usually attempt to curb through dieting?" An attempt will be made to examine this issue later in the book. Meanwhile, the gross overestimates which characterize many anorectics probably owe this extra distortion to several specific factors. (i) Their general wish to convey to others that they are more physically normal than is the case. (Experimentally it is possible to get anorectics to scale down their estimates of their fatness by reassuring them that a more realistic estimate will not jeopardize their defensive standing in relation to the experimenter/would-be therapist.) (ii) Their terror that, unless they can continue to curb their eating, they could become truly obese. They see themselves as they could rapidly become. Anorectics whose fragile low-weight control mechanisms have moved to a style of bingeing and vomiting are likely to suffer this experience most, along with a growing sense of imminent loss of control of eating.

Many anorectics live with a carefully concealed sense of panic which is more or less constant, especially during the early stages of the disorder or if they come to binge and vomit habitually. Such panic, partly contentless, is nevertheless also focussed on the possibility of gaining a little weight and hence also of eating anything substantial. If she gives in to the temptation to eat, especially if excessively, then the panic will become compounded by a sense of guilt, shame and disgust. At such times the anorectic is most despairing and potentially most self-destructive. Such concealed feelings are the more hard to bear since others are usually cheered at this stage by witnessing such behaviour or weight gain in the afflicted person.

Of course the ultimate irony for the anorectic—starving herself in the presence of plenty—is that, precisely because she is starved and hungry, she is preoccupied with thoughts of food and eating. All the biological forces still within her demand that she seek out food and consume it. As described earlier, this leads to much of her isolated and defensive behaviour within the household and in relation to mealtimes. Even during her few hours of sleep each day she will dream of food and its associations and consequences. One of the few things which may temporarily drive thoughts of food out of her mind is her school work, or her work at college or university if this is still her background. Many anorectics are anyway over-involved in seeking academic achievement and their capacity to work so hard, already facilitated by their regressed state, is further aided by the relief from thinking about food that concentrating on their work provides.

Some anorectics have an occasional experience of exhilaration or even ecstasy when they find that they are managing especially well to maintain their low weight. Feelings of triumph and rare contentment can also occasionally accompany secret bingeing, especially at night, when the individual concerned is secure in the knowledge not only that her eating will not be observed but that she will shortly be vomiting and eliminating the food and water from her body.

Many anorectics are aware that they are causing deep distress to parents or others close to them. However, they feel helpless to bridge the gulf between themselves and others—too much has to be concealed—too little can be understood and furthermore the starved state breeds a self-interest which is all-consuming.

Diagnosis

The attitude of the anorectic to the doctor or any other would-be helper ensures that the diagnosis of the condition is invariably difficult and sometimes can only be based on circumstantial evidence. It is usually helpful and indeed an elementary first step to seek and obtain information not only from the anorectic but also from others around her—members of the family, teachers, etc. Readily available information may be restricted by the major resistance of the girl to any kind of intervention directed solely at her gaining weight. As previously stated, other aspects of behaviour such as bingeing, vomiting, purging or the consumption of other pills designed to reduce weight (for example diuretics, amphetamine) may be totally concealed from would-be informants. Even the history of the dieting may be concealed, and in particular the underlying concern about shape and the now ever present terror or phobia of and need to avoid normal body weight. The previous history of dieting may even be denied by other members of the family but revealed by someone such as a teacher or a friend.

The anorectic often misleads people so completely that she can effectively manage to be under intense medical care and be painstakingly investigated into some facet of her disorder, e.g. unexplained diarrhoea and the question of whether or not this is due to excessive purgative ingestion, without the underlying diagnosis of "weight phobia" or "pursuit of thinness" being suspected.

The nature of the earlier adolescent turmoil, now condensed into and resolved by the anorectic stance, but still underpinning and maintaining the weight phobia, is usually well concealed, partly because of the powerful repressive forces at work within the family which are as operative now as they were at the time preceding the onset of the illness, and partly because the conflict is no longer real—the disorder has resolved it, and effectively divorced the anorectic from any normal and immediate experience of it in a psychobiological sense. So often, one is left merely with the physical findings, which are in many ways not specific to anorexia nervosa, but similar to the effects of weight loss from whatever cause, "psychological" or "physical", on which to base a presumptive diagnosis of the condition.

Laboratory Findings

The state of severe starvation is accompanied by a shut-down by the body of non-essential functions. Reproductive potential and full peripheral circulation are sacrificed. A new, conserving, residually essential lower metabolic activity supervenes early on. With the cessation of menstruation and its underlying hormonal mechanisms the body's energy expenditure falls by about 10%. As starvation becomes more severe, commonly in most subjects with a reduction in weight below about 6½ stones (92 lbs, 42 kgs) then there is a further step-like fall in resting metabolic activity with which the new low blood pressure, slow pulse rate, low body temperature and reversal of diurnal temperature rhythm are consonant. This new and often steady low resting metabolic state can be measured in the laboratory, for instance in terms of body heat generated or oxygen consumed per unit time. At such low weights the pituitary gland will also remain unresponsive to stimulation by hypothalamic releasing factors specific to pituitary reproductive hormone (LH/FSH) production. These natural biological adjustments only hold true for anorectics who are maintaining low body weight by the process of basic and selective abstinence from eating. The anorectic who, though low in body weight— say 5½ stones (77 lbs, 35 kgs)—is nevertheless bingeing and vomiting, apart from being in a radically different overall metabolic state, is also relatively and unnaturally "supercharged" in respect of her resting energy expenditure. In such a person the resting metabolic activity will be reduced by say 20% instead of by 40% as in the comparable-weight abstaining anorectic. Consonant with this unbiological state there will be a tendency to menstruate at lower than natural and normal body weight. For instance menstruation may return at a significantly lower level than it first arose and then was subsequently inhibited in that individual earlier in her life. Associated with this there will of course be relatively increased endocrine activity occurring at a lower body weight in respect of the hypothalamic/pituitary/ovarian axis. Such subjects do not provide a normal biological model for the pubertal process and for the usual kinds of starvation. Meanwhile the low levels of basic energy expenditure in anorectics appear to exist alongside a constant sense they have of restlessness which is such that they, as has previously been said, are rarely able to sit down or relax.

   The other metabolic abnormalities in anorexia nervosa in the main reflect the variety of dietetic patterns. Levels of lipid (fat) in the blood may be very high or low, probably depending on (i) the amount of fat being eaten. (ii) the periodicity of eating and the amount of carbohydrate ingested (e.g. some anorectics binge for a day or so every few weeks and otherwise eat hardly anything). Usually there will be low levels of glucose and high levels of insulin in the blood, but these will fluctuate in relation to specific episodes of ingestion of fat/carbohydrate, whether known by or hidden from others.

Anorectics do not become anaemic or deficient in the main essential elements and vitamins unless they have entered a phase of indiscriminate bingeing and vomiting. So long as they are in a primary and selective state of carbohydrate avoidance and starvation they may even eat an excess not only of fat but also of protein-containing foods, and can occasionally for instance poison themselves with protein degradation products which are produced in excess of the kidneys' capacity to excrete them. Occassionally, very high levels of carotene are consumed in certain vegetables, resulting in an orange tinged skin.

With the supervening of bingeing/vomiting/purging/consumption of diuretics type of low weight control, the general metabolic picture changes radically. It may be further complicated if punctuated by periods when the subject drinks excessive quantities of fluid in an effort to assuage hunger without consuming solid food. Severe dehydration may arise alternating with obvious dependent oedema—usually of course reflecting itself in ankle swelling. Electrolyte levels and balance within the body are severely disrupted and in the blood very low levels of potassium arise in association with massive purgation in particular.

Finally and in relation to the clinical finding that anorectics sleep little, especially during the second half of the night, the polygraphic recording of the EEG, muscle tone and eye movements during the night shows that in electrophysiological terms the anorectic has long periods of wakefulness especially during the second half of the night, and a corresponding major reduction in REM (dream) sleep.

Other Variants of Anorexia Nervosa — Atypical, Marginal and Convalescent Cases

Like many other "diseases", anorexia nervosa can blend both quantitatively and qualitatively with the normal. Atypical forms also exist. Individuals who are recovering show less of the features of the condition at all levels e.g. physical status, behaviour, experience. Others only ever develop it marginally and such minor episodes can often be picked up in the histories of people later in life.

Some anorectics who move towards apparent recovery in terms of regaining their weight nevertheless continue to have difficulty in controlling their food intake and may become obese and develop a state often described as "compulsive eating". In this they tend to go on periodic eating binges and often become or remain socially phobic, isolated individuals and very unhappy. They would seem to blend with a larger population of adolescent girls who have never dipped down into a classical anorexia nervosa and which, as a population, itself blends, in terms of the severity of the disorder, with the larger normal population.

Another group of girls, previously severely obese, sustain a more or less normal body weight—they often look normal and to all intents and purposes are accepted as normal by most others—but they only sustain their normal shape by vomiting in response to massive bingeing bouts. This behaviour may be entirely concealed or otherwise only known to a chosen flat mate. Such people, often as desperate as the underweight anorectic and just as preoccupied with their weight and its control, are nevertheless subject to powerful conflicts over their social and sexual roles, often alternating between phobically driven avoidance of contact with people on the one hand and impulsive sexual behaviour on the other. The nature of their relationships is invariably such that they are unhappy with them. Such people not infrequently go on to develop either classical anorexia nervosa or else obesity. Other potentially obese people sustain a normal body weight through rigid dietary control. Their sense of their own shape may or may not be distorted but their unnatural nutritional stance, with body weight held below its "set point" regulation leads, if firmly held, to menstrual irregularities; often to paucity or irregularity of menstrual periods. Such people also become preoccupied with their diet. Yet other people of normal body weight become excessively preoccupied with and seek a high degree of physical fitness allied to exact maintenance of an idealized "healthy" body weight throughout life. These latter types of eating pattern and weight control, though morbid in their extreme expression both in themselves and in their relationship to the total life style of the person concerned, need nevertheless to be clearly differentiated from anorexia nervosa.

3
Epidemiology and Natural History

Prevalence/Incidence

Although the condition has been most extensively described within the European, North American and Australasian medical literature, it has also been recorded as present in other parts of the world and in other cultures. I have even seen it in severe form in the Arab/Moslem world. In recent years medical writers have begun to report large series of cases (50 or more) and these include reports from Russia and eastern European countries as well as from the West.

In Britain in particular it has been suggested that the disorder has become more common in the last decade. This is almost certainly the case, although both the recognition of it in society and more accurate diagnosis within the clinic have also contributed to this effect. Those few medical clinics which specialize in treating it are inundated with referrals. At present I receive requests to see new patients at the rate of over 20 per week, only one of which can be accepted.

The condition appears to be more common in the southern part of this country, possibly because of its association with social class. One recent study of schoolgirls revealed that, within the independent sector of education it is present in severe form in one in every 100 females aged 16 to 18 years inclusive. Such schools encountered one severe new case per year amongst every 250 girls. Within the 16 to 18 age bracket in the State educational system it is much less common—about one in every 300 such girls. This discrepancy again probably reflects the fundamentally different incidence between the social classes which has also been noted in the clinic populations reported by various workers—with the condition having until now been more common amongst families in the professional and managerial range of occupations so far as the father is concerned.

This skewed distribution of morbidity, in which the working class background seems to have a sparing effect, is unusual in respect of disease, although the same phenomenon is found with a few other disorders; for instance migraine, which may also have direct clinical affinities with anorexia nervosa, and may even now be changing. It is my impression that the disorder is now becoming relatively more common in what for want of a better term are called lower middle class and working class families. Possible reasons for this are given later in the book.

The disorder may be even more common in a slightly older age bracket than that systematically studied above; many researchers have found the average age of onset to be about 18 years. Some staff health services of universities and colleges catering for the 18–21 year old bracket, have described the condition as being present in almost epidemic proportions amongst the female student population. It appears to be particularly common amongst some groups, those engaged in such subjects as, for instance, nutrition, sport, ballet, fashion, modelling, except when wary authorities have selected out such would-be appointees. Thus people who already have the condition are attracted to such occupations as these.

The presence of such severe, undoubted and identified cases within the population is complemented by an even greater number of mild, incipient, convalescent and hidden cases.

Natural History

It is possible to state one's impression of the natural evolution of the condition but any such views must be hedged around by qualifications. For instance, it is usually only possible to comment systematically on the course that the disorder has pursued amongst those people with it who have attended hospital and have thus been identified and documented and are then available for follow-up studies some years later. A few such careful studies have been reported. Other similar attempts have turned out to have limited value because not all individuals could be traced. Even when comprehensively studied in follow-up, such populations may not represent the majority of affected persons. Many such people will have received treatment which may or may not have influenced outcome. They are also likely, on the whole, to represent that segment of the anorectic population judged to be the most ill; for instance, being severely emaciated or obviously odd in their behaviour. It is not all that uncommon to encounter women in middle life who, although now sometimes less than well in some other respect, describe an episode of anorexia nervosa in their teens which lasted a few months or a year or two and in respect of which they received no attention from doctors or others.

Meanwhile, in respect of that group which has passed through the medical/psychiatric clinic culture, the following things can be said.

The disorder emerges within the context of or following the biological process of puberty. As I hope to show in subsequent chapters it is these events of puberty that confer the new important meaning on body shape and weight which is the core of anorexia nervosa. Puberty, as a process, occurs over a period of many months and the first menstrual bleed is a late feature. It is thus that the disorder can occasionally erupt before the menarche and thereby be associated with primary amenorrhoea in the female.

Usually, however, the condition supervenes later in adolescence and, as has been previously stated, the average age of onset has almost always been found to be around 17–18 years of age.

The concept of age-of-onset presupposes some universally agreed marker or indicant for onset of the condition. In fact investigators have used various criteria, and the complexity of the situation has been compounded by the common propensity of the established anorectic to effectively conceal aspects of her history surrounding the development of the condition. Attempts at retrospective documentation of the development of the condition such as commonly have to occur in the clinic are therefore liable to lead to the production of patchy and inaccurate information, especially in relation to the centrally important areas. Indeed, information gathered from other and independent sources is fundamental to careful initial clinical enquiry in this condition.

Early on in the evolution of the condition there is a sense of being fat and a wish to reduce this feeling. This experience is widespread amongst the female adolescent population, and although it becomes very intense in the anorectic-to-be it would not appear to be qualitatively different at this stage from the more universal experience. The emergence of anorexia nervosa in relation to it owes a great deal to other factors as well as the increasingly special importance of fatness for the individual concerned. The underlying meanings of fatness in adolescence in general and for the anorectic in particular will be explored in some detail later. For the present purposes of describing the course of the illness it is suffficient to say that a certain degree of plumpness at this stage is common amongst those destined to develop anorexia nervosa, but it is by no means essential. Relatedly, as a population, anorectics will be found to have achieved puberty earlier than others. Thus, pubertal and early post-pubertal plumpness is associated with rapid growth through childhood. However, once again, such growth characteristics are neither obligatory for, nor, of course, exclusive to the development of the condition.

A few anorectics seem to have had a relatively late puberty although, in such cases, it is always important to remember the possibility of an earlier episode of the condition having occurred which has then blighted or stifled an otherwise early puberty or at least an early menarche. If this latter is the case there may have been hints of a phase of plumpness, early breast development etc. as early as eight or nine years of age but which then ceased, only to be rekindled in an attenuated form and with perhaps a brief phase of menstruation before the onset of the second episode of anorexia nervosa. This second episode is then more likely to be characterized by overeating and vomiting as the means of low weight control, in contrast perhaps to the earlier and concealed phase associated with abstinence.

Returning to consideration of the initial onset of the condition, the individual's increasing preoccupation with fatness, often itself kept secret, although if associated with plumpness then almost invariably associated with teasing by others, will have led to her attempting to diet i.e. to restrict daily calorie consumption. Invariably this takes the form of restricting carbohydrate. Such behaviour often precedes the obvious onset of anorexia nervosa for months or years. However occasionally such preoccupation and behaviour only develop immediately before the onset. Under these circumstances the individual often becomes obviously sensitized to her shape following an interlude such as Christmas, which is not infrequently associated with family feasting and with weight gain, or a first holiday away from the family when she gained weight. Such weight gains, based on the change in constraints, and in the last instance also being associated with being away from home, often contain within them in explicit form a common core ingredient of the genesis of anorexia nervosa, the association in the subject's and the family's mind between eating on the one hand and adolescent social and sexual behaviour on the other. If this association exists either in the family's fantasy or in reality, for instance if the holiday has been associated not only with overeating but with a first tentative or more intimate contact with boys, then a reaction against the latter may take the form of a sudden determination to banish the newfound fatness and all that it represents, both in terms of general femininity and also more concretely sometimes the contour of early pregnancy.

The definite onset of anorexia nervosa is heralded by an intensification of dieting both in a calorific and social sense. All carbohydrate is avoided, extreme fussiness over eating supervenes, she becomes increasingly secretive and given to acute distress or trantrums if not allowed to control conditions surrounding her eating and the aftermath of meals when she may need to go off and vomit. She may begin to take over the family cooking at this stage. Weight loss is sometimes dramatic, especially the fall say from 8 to 6½ stones (112–92 lbs, 51–41 kgs).

Menstruation often ceases at an early stage and may be more readily accepted by others as the first symptom than is the individual's attitude to shape and consequent dieting.

To give an idea of the association of anorexia nervosa with obesity, it can be said on the basis of a recent extensive survey that, as a population, anorectics have a premorbid weight of around 9½ stones (133 lbs, 60 kgs), but with a scatter around this average such that the standard deviation is 1 stone 11 lbs (25 lbs, 11 kgs).

Thus approximately 70 per cent of anorectics have a pre-illness weight within the range 7 stone 10 lbs to 11 stone 4 lbs (108–158 lbs, 50–72 kgs). This compares with an average weight of 8 stone 10 lbs ± 9 lbs for the comparable non-anorectic population. The average weight of the anorectic at the time of her last menstrual period is 8 stone 3 lbs ± 13 lbs, i.e. for 70% of the population the last menstrual period occurs within the range of 7 stone 4 lbs to 9 stone 2 lbs (102–128 lbs, 46–58 kgs). (In the fullness of time this will also be the weight at which her menstruation returns if she recovers to this extent.)

Thereafter the anorectic may continue to lose weight, but usually weight plateaus for a while. Further sudden losses are often associated with episodes construed by others as "tummy upsets" or "gastric flu" etc. but which usually reflect some near loss of control of her low body weight by the anorectic. Thus she may have begun to binge secretly, creating great panic within herself as well as abdominal discomfort. She may have vomited in reaction to this or resorted to purgatives, and over the week or so of the crisis the outcome may be substantial further weight loss. The episode may even have been associated with an apparent high body temperature—in fact the product of the gorging. Occasionally an episode of very heavy overeating leads to a sleepy state, into which the anorectic then retreats with relief, presenting thereby with a stuporose or comatose-like condition which invites a differential diagnosis of encephalitis. If such a diagnosis is mistakenly made then the subsequent dietetic disorder often comes to be attributed to the now wrongly presumed brain damage.

At this stage also the anorectic may be eating normal or even excessive amounts of protein, fruit, cheese and other similar foods. Figures 1–8 show the typical dietetic pattern of anorectics at this stage compared with the pattern of non-anorectic females. It should be remembered that although Group B and C anorectics (who binge) are shown to consume large quantities of food at times, at the end of the day they have vomited most of it.

Those around the anorectic will by now usually have observed that she has broken off her contact with friends, especially any boyfriends who had been important. If she is still at school her work performance may even be improving as she increasingly commits herself to study.

The restlessness previously referred to is common, especially at night when it may lead to waking up in the morning much earlier than is usual. Such restlessness may take the form of strenuous exercise as the anorectic strives still more to maintain her low weight or else diminish it further.

Unlike the person who has lost appetite the anorectic often betrays her sustained though denied hunger through her continued preoccupation with food. Sooner or later she may surrender to the impulse to eat. Her terror is that, once started she may never stop, and so she will become hideously and shamefully fat. Some anorectics nevertheless fall victim to such impulses and binge their way miserably out of their low weight state. They may then present later as isolated, socially phobic, overweight adolescents and be labelled as "compulsive eaters". Others may still regain weight but without such an overswing—they will usually be characterized by not having been voracious eaters or obese before the illness. Others, however, especially if obesity seems the only alternative, may resort to vomiting for the first time at this stage.

Many anorectics, probably more than half, resort to this mechanism of weight control at some stage, albeit briefly. Perhaps 30% of all anorectics, however, finish up with this as an habitual means of weight control. Now many foods, including large quantities of carbohydrate, may be consumed indiscriminately. Vomiting this then leads to a more general protein-calorie deprivation and starvation, and to dehydration and loss of important electrolytes. Such a pattern is also the most common way in which anorectics come to consume large quantities of

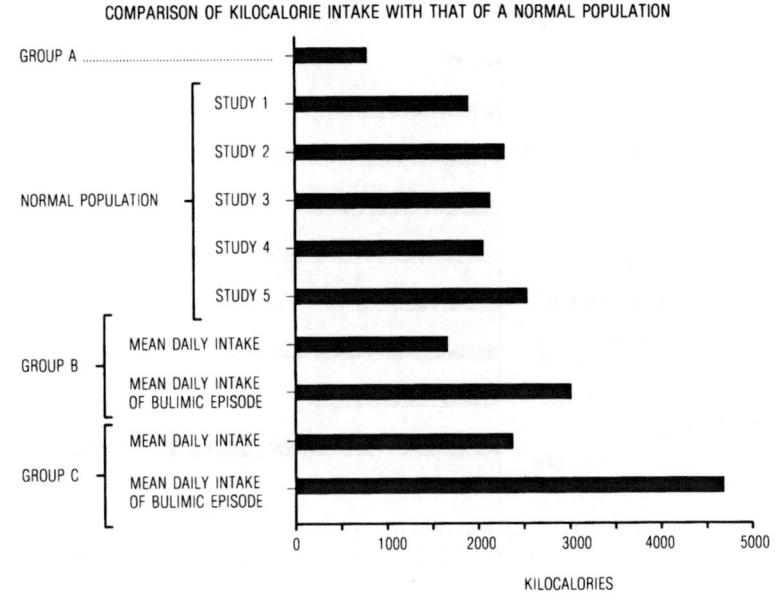

Fig. 1

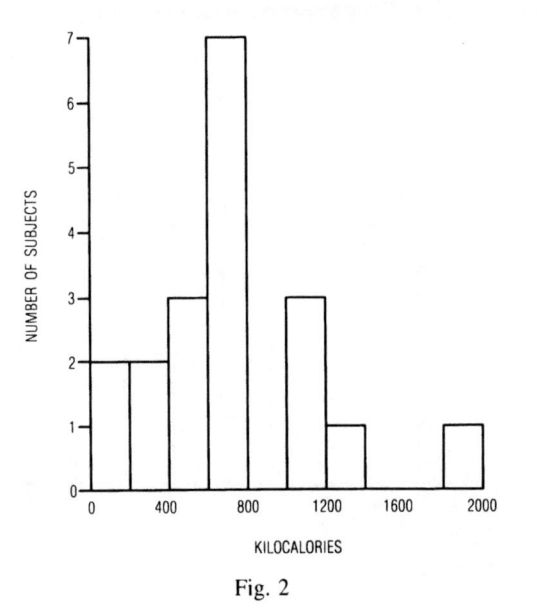

Fig. 2

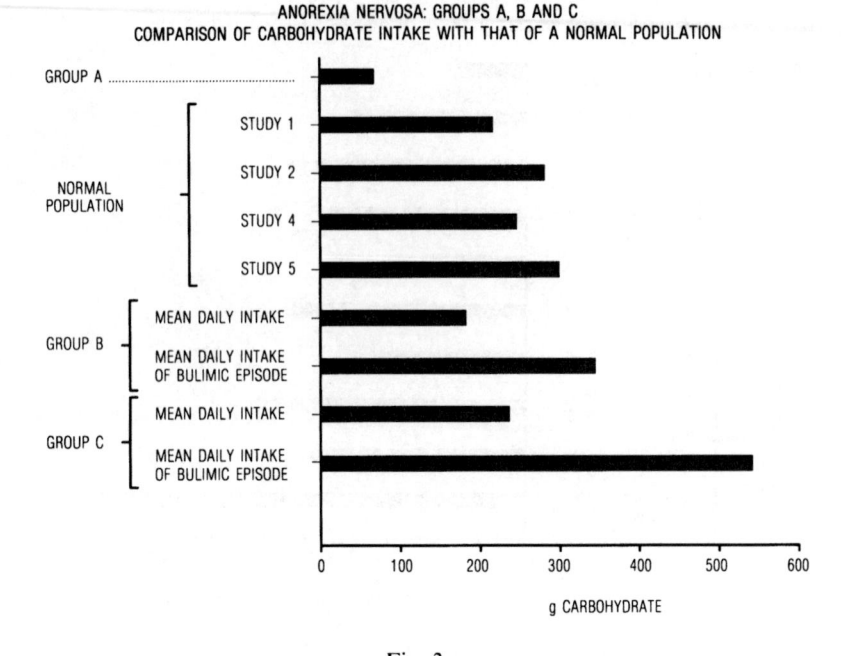

ANOREXIA NERVOSA: GROUPS A, B AND C
COMPARISON OF CARBOHYDRATE INTAKE WITH THAT OF A NORMAL POPULATION

Fig. 3

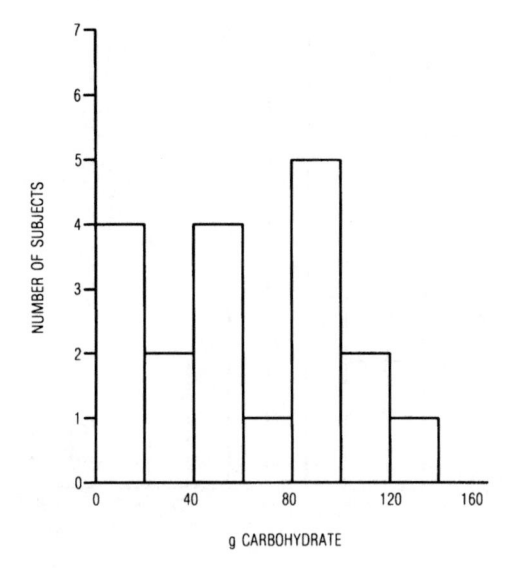

19 SUBJECTS WITH ANOREXIA NERVOSA IN GROUP A TO SHOW
DISTRIBUTION OF CARBOHYDRATE INTAKE WITHIN THIS GROUP

Fig. 4

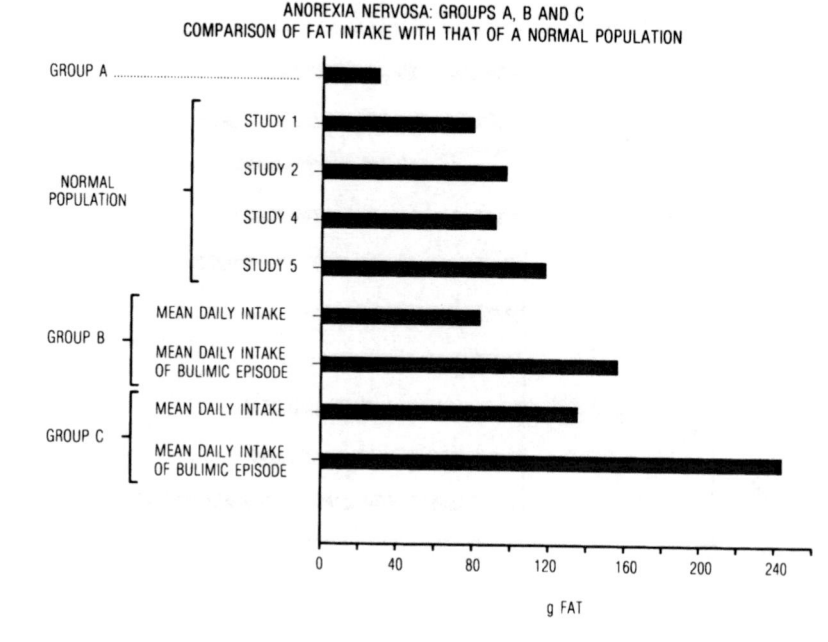

Fig. 5

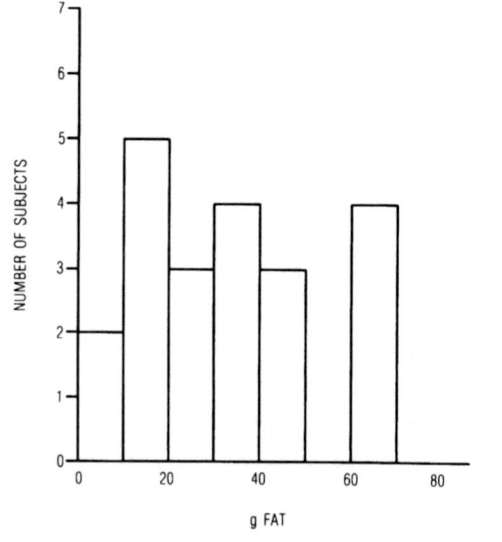

Fig. 6

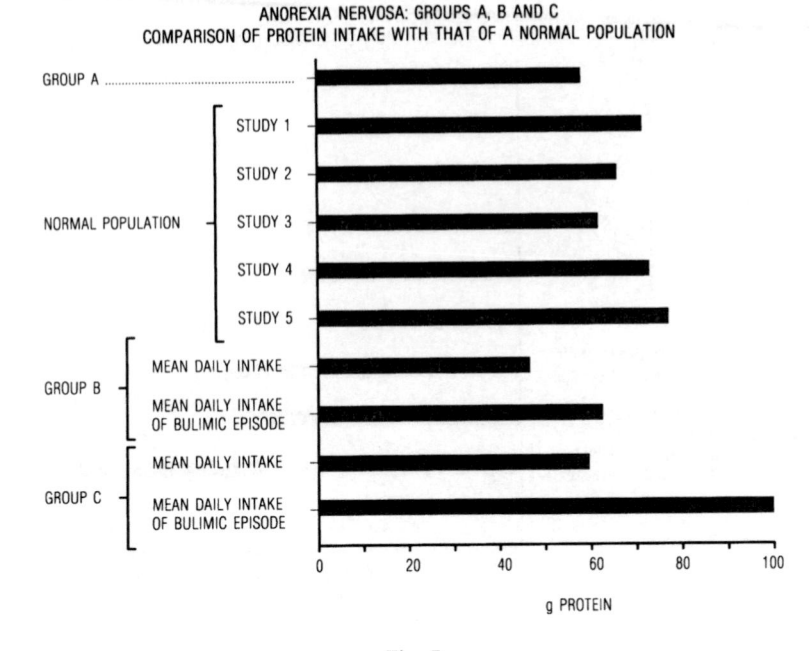

Fig. 7

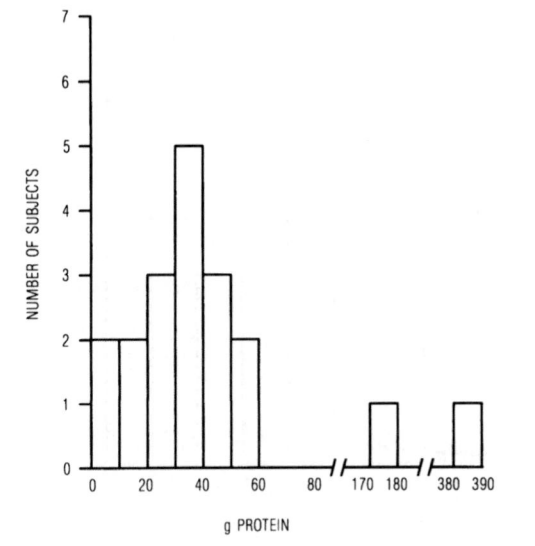

Fig. 8

purgatives. The particularly severe constipation associated with vomiting provides the basis for this. It is not uncommon for such anorectics to consume dozens of Senacot tablets, or, less commonly, large quantities of other purgatives, daily. This consumption is arrived at by the anorectic as she struggles to retain her low weight and finds that the watery diarrhoea that predictably follows purgation leads to some small weight loss which will provide her with a sense of relief and the courage to once again check her weight on the scales. Such purgation has further sinister consequences on physical health. Now she will lose further precious protein, fluid and potassium in particular in her stool. Gross chemical disturbances arise in the body which can facilitate such disorders as acute gastric dilatation and epilepsy as well as other neurological disorders and cardiac crises. Further weight loss down to a level of body weight of about 4½ to 5½ stones (63–77 lbs, 29–35 kgs) often occurs. It is surprising how many such anorectics can survive (occasionally for instance with a plasma potassium level of lower than two millimols per litre for many years on end). They also show remarkable resistance to infection right until the end. Death, which occurs in about 5% of them, is due either to suicide or occurs through some complication of the severe inanition e.g. potassium depletion or the ultimate total absence of energy supplies. Whereas official records indicate that 20–30 individuals in the United Kingdom die from anorexia nervosa each year, it is the case that the number is substantially more than this since such deaths are not infrequently recorded as due to suicide. To the end such anorectics will protest their normality and claim not to feel thin, let alone emaciated.

Although it has been stated above that anorectics occasionally recover after a few months, this is rare. More usually the illness lasts several years. Recovery can occasionally be followed by relapse (typically following a pregnancy). Otherwise chronicity over many years can be compatible with survival. Such people if they are abstainers tend to be isolated and frugal in all aspects of their life—they are often engaged in

---

FIGS 1–8. Selective restrictions of diet in anorexia nervosa. Group A individuals are those who abstain from eating. Their overall calorie intake is significantly less (Fig. 1) than that of normal subjects (Studies 1–5 reflect dietary surveys carried out on five distinct "normal" young adult female populations), and this restriction is mainly of carbohydrate (Fig. 3) and to a lesser extent of fat (Fig. 5). Indeed it can be seen that two individuals consumed very large quantities of protein (Fig. 8). Groups B and C respectively comprise anorectics who binge infrequently and frequently, and who also vomit in relation to such bingeing. Their actual assimilation of calories is often less than that amongst the Group A abstainers.

the food industry in some form or other. Chronically ill bingers and vomiters have a different fate. Even at low body weight they often feel alternately very energetic and otherwise listless. They live in constant fear that their appetite will take them over. Biologically they are in a highly abnormal state, with a much higher level of basal metabolism than is consonant with their degree of starvation. Even at low body weights they may occasionally find themselves sexually preoccupied. Although rarely getting any satisfaction or contentment from sexual relationships they may plunge into them recklessly from time to time. They can sometimes regain fertility at quite low body weights, and one sometimes comes across anorectics who have obviously been severely ill for many years but have become pregnant on one or more occasions when their weight increased a little, say up to around 6½ stones (91 lbs, 41 kgs). Anorectics in this state of constant bingeing and vomiting often develop a sustained yearning to have things in their mouth and may become chain smokers, may turn to alcohol or other drugs. Sometimes in an effort to assuage their hunger without consuming calories they will drink very large quantities of water, which then further complicates their physical state. Since such anorectics may continue to maintain much of their behaviour in secret they present the most complex diagnostic puzzles to doctors when for some reason or another they reach them. The differential diagnosis of the kind of clinical and metabolic problem that these patients present is often a great challenge and misdiagnosis is common.

So far it has been inferred that the condition always starts in adolescence i.e. in that period between puberty and the late teens. This is not so. Indeed the mean age of onset of 17 or 18 years ± 5 years shows that in a number of instances the disorder first erupts in the early twenties. Very rarely it can arise for the first time even later in life. However, in this latter circumstance, in most instances it will be found that the condition represents a relapse, having first occurred in the individual's teens, this then being followed by a period of recovery. When the condition genuinely supervenes later in life then it is much more likely to be associated with a major degree of premorbid obesity. The obese person is likely to have been struggling to reduce weight for years and may indeed have lost some down to near normal or normal levels, but only at the price of vigorous dietary control. Only later does anorexia nervosa emerge. Under such conditions it can be seen that, whatever age she may be at the time of onset, she has been wrestling with problems of an adolescent order.

It has already been stated that anorexia nervosa is a condition from which people can recover spontaneously. Given all the complicating factors concerning identification of individuals with the condition, it will be realized that it is hard to say anything substantial or definitive about outcome in statistical terms. However it is now beginning to seem that, at least so far as severe cases are concerned, approximately 40% of such individuals can expect to be free of the condition five or six years later. Of course this begs the question what is meant by "free of the condition".

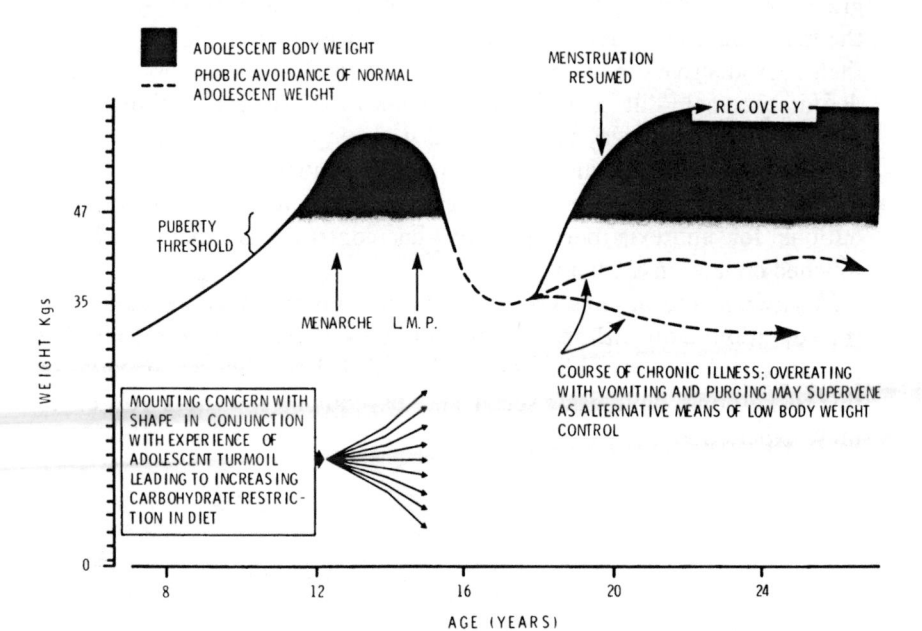

FIG. 9. The evolution of anorexia nervosa is shown in diagrammatic form in this figure. The threshold weights, shown in representative form here, reflect significant stages of sexual maturation within the pubertal processes around which the disorder pivots. Established anorexia nervosa is rooted in the need to maintain body weight and shape below this threshold—a task which demands maintenance of what is inherently biologically a most unstable position and constantly subject to the natural thrust of early pubertal growth and related appetite. In the face of this constant threat of weight gain through the threshold, the anorectic retreats into increasingly low body weight and becomes ever more terrified of any slight weight gain reflecting and revealing to others her loss of control over the situation. Only if she has absolute control over the maintenance of her body weight at a barely sub-pubertal level, for which the mechanism of freely vomiting usually needs to be available, may she then honestly claim that, indeed, she does not wish to lose more weight. Under these circumstances her adult body weight phobia will be even less detectable than usual, and only revealed in a situation in which she loses authority over her current delicate weight control mechanisms.

Some such people will for instance by then have a normal weight but may either be maintaining this in an abnormal way so far as diet is concerned, or they may still feel very distressed about their shape, to such an extent for instance that it severely hampers their social life. Their menstruation will have returned but their personal relationships may remain somewhat limited (Fig. 9).

But what eventually happens to those chronically disabled anorectics who do not die from their condition. This is truly an "elephants' graveyard" mystery—we do not know. Some remit at around the time of the menopause after having the condition since puberty—it has spanned their reproductive life and at the end of this time it is shed. Some others definitely remain "ill" with it. Amenorrhoea is no longer a hallmark and they survive as isolated, eccentric and wizened old ladies. However, we have no systematic information as to its course in later life.

It is my view that treatment of certain kinds can improve the long term outlook for anorexia nervosa, but this controversial matter will be touched on later in the book.

Meanwhile, the emphasis so far has been to insist that anorexia nervosa is a condition to do with the meaning of body shape and weight, and that it arises out of puberty. The next section of the book focusses on some of the background biological, social and psychological factors related to these experiences.

SECTION II
Background to the Disorder

This section of the book is concerned with some of the factors that predispose the individual to the development of anorexia nervosa on passing into or through puberty.

The initiation of many diseases can be thought of in terms of some immediate precipitant interacting with constitutional factors within the individual. In the classical disease model it is a potentially pathological organism, for instance a bacterium, interacting with its host. The state of resistance of the host will govern whether or not a disease erupts and in what form this happens. An apparently chance accident, for instance being struck by a car, will often owe something to the victim's nature. For instance is he depressed and uncaring, is he obese and sluggish, is he preoccupied with other matters, is he blind or deaf? Yet again some clinicians believe that the emergence of an active malignant process against a background of vulnerability to such growth, is triggered by some immediate trauma or stress. In my view anorexia nervosa stems from the coming together of such constitutional (long standing) and experiential (immediate experience) factors. This section is concerned with identifying some of these. For the sake of simplicity it deals with them as if they are separate processes when in fact this is not the case. Thus the significance of a precipitating experience stems not only from the absolute and specific intensity of the stimulus but also from its meaning to the individual, which in turn usually owes a great deal both to the social context and to the person's previous biological and social experience, and hence to her development and her consequent resources. Such constitutional factors will be reflected both in the individual's bodily characteristics and her personality.

It will come to be seen that many of the factors that contribute to the disorder are not specific or unique to it. They appear to exist in other persons, both in their constitutional and experiential aspects. They can be seen as "risk" factors and it would seem to be their coming together in certain ways that leads to the experience and associated behaviour which is specific to the condition—namely the avoidance of normal adult body weight by the maintenance of low body weight control in association with an overwhelming panic at the prospect of any weight gain.

4
Childhood Bodily Growth and the Pubertal Process

In the General Population

Babies weigh about 6–8 lbs (3–4 kg) at birth. The birth weights of babies born of any one mother increase with parity, and such later born babies are, like only children, more likely to be obese in adult life. During growth to puberty, body weight will increase at least tenfold whilst height will increase nearly threefold. During this same period shape changes. The relative sizes of head, trunk and limbs change considerably and changes also occur during childhood in the amount of fat within the body. These latter changes are of course most evident in respect of the fat deposited under the skin and thereby lending contour to the body. The thickness of subcutaneous fat normally increases during the first year of life and then decreases to reach a minimum at about six years of age. Following this there is a steady increase in body fat as puberty is approached.

Speed of growth is highly variable between children. However, overall there is a slowing down in rate of increase in height as puberty is approached. The slowest rate of weight gain, however, is often during the second and third years of life and after this there is some slight acceleration.

At birth the head is already 60% or so of its mature circumference. In contrast the legs, even at seven years of age, are only about 50% of their mature length. There is therefore a relative increase in limb size and decrease in head size in relation to overall bulk during growth.

As a general rule fatness in childhood is associated with rapid growth and with fatness in adult life although there are many exceptions to this, not the least of which, of course, is the emergence in biological maturity, of anorexia nervosa in a previously obese person.

The onset of puberty is characterized by a renewed spurt in growth, manifest most obviously in terms of a height spurt. This arises, on average, approximately two years earlier in girls than in boys although there is considerable variability in both sexes in this respect. The earlier puberty starts, the shorter the person is ultimately destined to be. Thus, on average, physically mature females are also shorter than physically mature men. This is in contrast to the fact that, prior to such an early puberty, the individual will if anything have been taller than her peers.

There is a great deal of evidence that, at least in the female (the menarche has always been a useful indicator and measure of the timing of female puberty) puberty has arisen at an increasingly young age over the past century. Some evidence now suggests that it may have plateaued in this respect. This optimizing of childhood growth potential has probably been achieved through the eradication of chronic childhood infectious diseases and through the increasingly universal availability of adequate nutrition (not infrequently these days accompanied by overfeeding).

Puberty is characterized by a sustained acceleration and final phase of overall growth accompanied by the development of secondary sexual characteristics. The process lasts approximately four years. In boys it usually starts at some time between the ages of 11 and 15 years. In girls it starts somewhat earlier and is also more evident at this early stage.

Thus, the first indicator in girls, apart from the earlier height spurt, is the beginning of breast development. Next, pubic hair begins to appear, hips begin to increase in size, and subcutaneous fat deposition on buttocks, anterior abdomen, thighs, upper arms etc. in particular confer the typical biological mature contour. Axillary hair is a later development. Such changes are dependent upon the newly emerging female sex hormone pattern and it has been suggested that this female fatness has important biological significance in evolutionary terms, as well as its social significance. Any fatness present in the pubescent boy is less intimately a feature of the pubertal processes. Although it can be shown that boys do increase their fat deposition during this period the increase is modest and, for instance, at a height of 5 ft 11 ins (180 cm) fat mass averages 20 lbs (9 kgs). In contrast a girl of similar height would on average contain 44 lbs (20 kgs) of fat. In contrast to the hip development of the pubescent female, in the male there is a major increase in shoulder width, as part of a male-based proportionately greater increase in lean body mass at this stage.

The first menstrual bleed in the female usually occurs late in the pubertal process. Even in their third year of puberty not all girls have started to menstruate. Indeed the onset of menstruation heralds a rapid decrease in growth rate and a cessation of growth within a year or so. Cyclical ovulation and regular menstruation is normally established within the two years beyond the menarche.

In boys puberty is further characterized by an increase in size of the external genitalia, the development of pubic hair and, late in the pubertal process, a breaking of the voice and the development of axillary and facial hair.

The Hormonal Basis of Puberty

An intact hypothalamic pituitary gonadal/adrenal system is necessary for the process of puberty. The pituitary gonadotrophic hormones, luteinizing hormone and follicular stimulating hormone, which in the adult govern the monthly activity cycle of the ovaries, exist only in very small amounts in the blood of children. Early puberty is characterized by a rise in the level of these hormones, especially during sleep. The trigger to this development is unknown though it has been postulated that there exists a precise body weight and per cent body fatness threshold which is necessary for the initiation of the process. It is, of course, an overriding biological principle that the capacity to reproduce is contingent upon adequate growth to the point of maturity, and thereafter food intake remains necessary only to maintain the mature organism plus its offspring in their early development. It is therefore likely that, for a given species characterized by a certain mature size, this process will be reflected in such a weight/fatness threshold.

In particular it has been suggested that the high level of fat within the female reflects the evolutionary need for an adequate calorific reservoir to meet the growth requirements of the foetus and newborn infant given the unpredictable nature of environmental food supplies. To this extent such fatness is largely redundant for the contemporary western female, although, for many of us, it obviously continues to have great social and experiential significance, most of all of course for the anorectic.

In Anorexia Nervosa

There does not appear to be any unique or necessary quality to childhood growth in those destined to develop anorexia nervosa. Anorectics may

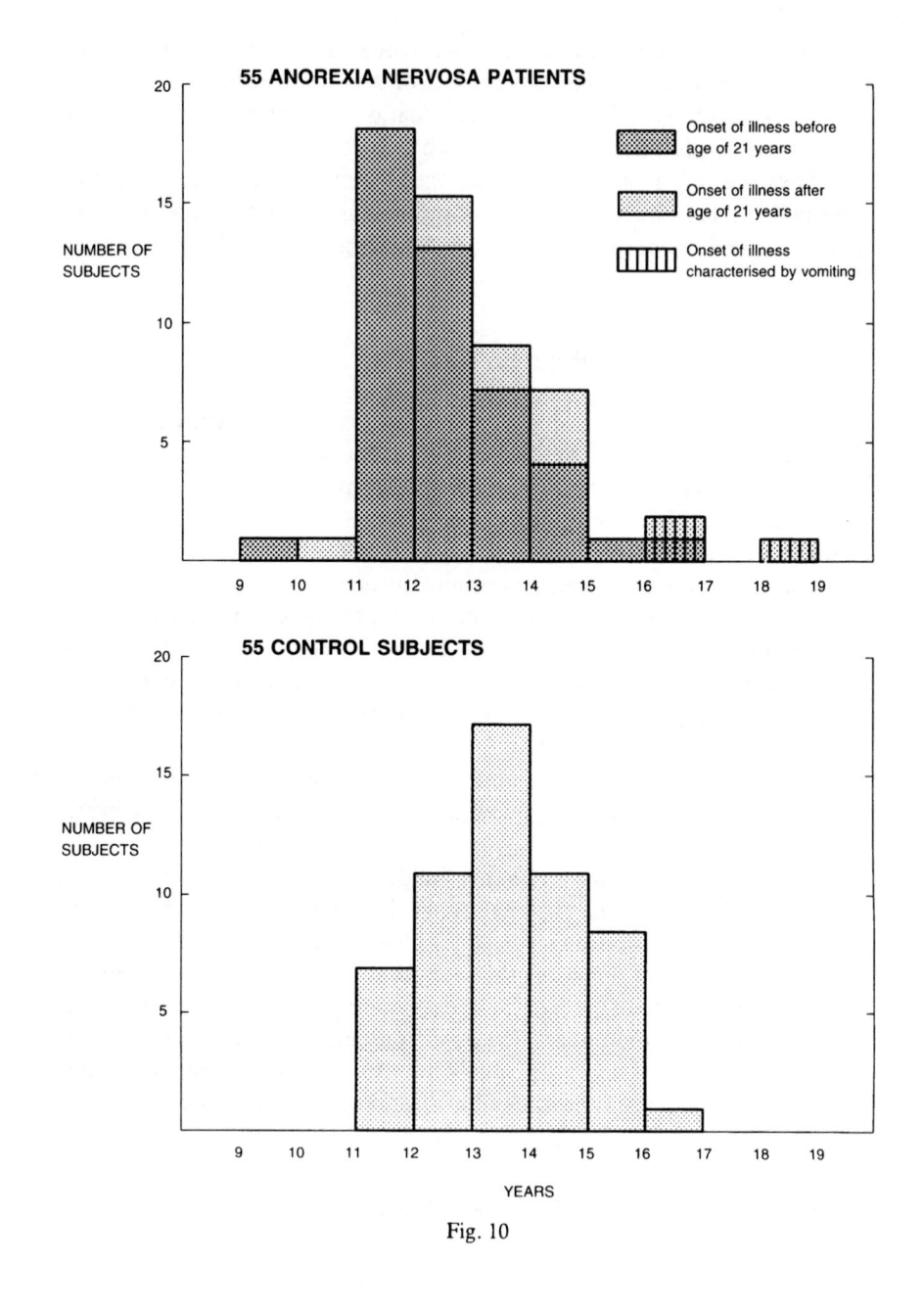

Fig. 10

have been skinny or certainly not plump as children. However, statistically speaking, fatness and high growth rate occur more commonly amongst them than others.

Even if childhood has not been associated with fatness then the early puberty will often have been associated with incipient plumpness to which the anorectic in particular will become very sensitive. Figure 10 shows this skewing towards rapid growth in an anorectic population.

The origins of such rapid growth, when it occurs, and its implications for the person with anorexia nervosa, are inevitably complex. There is a tendency for anorexia nervosa to occur in later born children within a family, and as such for them to weigh more at birth and to be more likely than others to be obese as adults. However, not all are later born and some are under average weight at birth.

The amount of food eaten, for one reason or another, in early life may, then, be a factor influencing growth as will be discussed later.

FIG. 10. These two charts allow comparison of the age of menarche of a group of anorectics with that of a group of normal subjects. The lower figure shows a normal distribution of age of puberty with the majority experiencing their first menstrual bleed during their thirteenth year, and with fewer having this experience either earlier or later. Amongst the anorectics an early menarche is more common, reflecting a higher rate of growth during childhood and greater pubertal fatness. Although this state of affairs is more common in anorexia nervosa it is by no means obligatory, and it can be seen that substantial numbers of anorectics do normally have late menarches, especially, in fact, those in whom the disorder developed at a later age. Although in three anorectics the disorder seems to have started with vomiting, one with a very early menarche and two with apparently very late menarches, it may be that this reflects their insistent report to others that only at this stage did they themselves feel apprehensive and seek help, probably in relation to underlying bingeing and threatened loss of control of their state. Thus it may be, with the two anorectics with a late menarche, that this reflected a previous period of anorexia nervosa maintained securely by abstaining and starting early in puberty, thereby smothering a natural early menarche.

5
Childhood Eating and Social Experiences

Although the insistence in this book is upon the primacy of body shape rather than food and eating as a determinant of anorexia nervosa, the reader will already be aware that food is intricately interwoven with growth and puberty, as well as human interaction in a variety of ways. Moreover, the family feeding patterns during childhood will reveal much about other important attitudes in it which will still be relevant to the adolescent period. Indeed it is a paradox, for instance, that many over-protective families investing in abundant nourishment of their children, may thereby precipitate them prematurely into biological maturity, and fat with it, whilst failing to equip them to cope with the social pressures consequent on it.

This chapter will therefore concern itself with aspects of feeding and eating in infancy, childhood and puberty.

In the General Population

Social organization among animals is governed by the need to secure food—which may include the need to defend territory. Primitive human societies are obviously similarly based. Our complex modern society has food supplies so well organized, and has such predictable and ensured patterns of daily activity and meals, that it might be thought that we could afford to relegate personal involvement with food and with mealtimes to a secondary place. That this is not so is a reflection of the complex social and psychological meanings that food has come to have.

The symbolism of food in our present day culture is almost too widespread for ready classification, and can be unique to the individual or his subculture. The family, and the mother in particular, are usually the earliest sources of food for the infant, and food can come to have important meanings to do with love, rejection, security and unity. It bears a relationship in the infant to growth and to health, and tends to become equated with these things in people's minds. Having contributed to lowering the age of puberty through its influence on the rate of growth, it thereafter continues to bear a complex biological and psychological relationship to sexual behaviour, and may increasingly assume moral significance.

Many aspects of behaviour such as smelling, seeing, hearing, attacking, foraging, biting, operate in relation to feeding behaviour. Such activities in the young animal, and the developing human infant too, are known to have centres of organization and interrelation in the visceral brain. This is a system of connected centres deep in the substance of the brain. It appears to have evolved initially in relation to the sense of smell. However, the more primitive "off-on switch" for feeding behaviour appears to be located even more deeply in the brain. This is a region which is intimately connected with the visceral brain and with the pituitary gland which in turn is related to the rest of the hormone gland system, and with that part of the nervous system that controls many of the internal organs of the body. In many species there appear to be separate tracts in this hypothalamic area concerned respectively with "hunger" and "satiety". If one set is destroyed experimentally then excessive eating results; if the other, then the animal does not eat even though food is plentiful and it is evidently malnourished. In natural existence it seems likely that these systems operate in harness and are sensitive to the chemical status of the body's nutrition, for example, to the level of sugar in the blood. Hunger, which is often experienced as a sensation in the abdomen, may also be signalled to the brain by the muscular activity and perhaps chemical secretions of the intestines and, of course, when the stomach is empty. This kind of feedback mechanism, whereby behaviour responds to chemical information, is basic throughout the range of biological life. In the human, the system is very complex indeed; after only a few days' carbohydrate starvation the body chemistry becomes disturbed for several weeks before settling down again to a normal routine.

Furthermore, in the human at least, activities of the visceral brain are likely to be influenced by ideas and feelings associated with other parts of the brain. Thus not only the actual smell but the idea of food may lead to hunger. Then, one step further, experimenters have discovered that the experience of being rejected by one's fellows is often followed by hunger feelings.

Food intake and body weight and shape are inextricably related in the individual from his earliest months of existence. During his first nine months of life he lives inside his mother's womb and derives his nourishment entirely from her. His nurture is governed by the mother's feeding habits and these will reflect her own lifelong pattern of feeding and perhaps her attitude to pregnancy. Such long-term maternal feeding habits are one factor related to the birth-weight of the offspring and this may contribute to the increase in birth-weight of babies as maternal age advances. Pregnancy is a time when a woman sometimes begins to eat in unusual ways, savouring foods which she usually avoids. This may have an immediate chemical basis in the developing pregnancy; certainly the combined metabolic needs of herself and her foetus are greater than those of herself alone. However, her changing feeding habits may also be dependent upon the psychological consequences of pregnancy—the way in which it is affecting her personal life, her marital and other family relationships—and also her fear of labour. She may feel it as a time during which she can relax her dietary control, usually aimed at keeping her slim and attractive. Now she has an excuse to eat and the weight gain may either be attributed by others directly to the pregnancy or else be approved of as proper under the circumstances. In this way many women gain weight in a step-like way with successive pregnancies.

Finally, she will be developing an attitude to the baby she is carrying. It may or may not have been planned or now be desired. It may have more relevance to her or her partner's general or marital security than to anything else. Her general needs to nourish those around her may be affected accordingly. In the early months of an undesired pregnancy some mothers starve themselves in the half-hope of aborting. Others, aware of their mixed feelings, may compensate by attempting to over-nourish their foetus. As the pregnancy proceeds, anxiety and depression may develop and produce either over or under-eating. Such habits during the last three months of pregnancy significantly affect the baby's growth before birth. In such ways, the baby already reflects in terms of his birth-weight and shape, and his body chemistry, the relationship between him and his mother.

However, the feeding habits of his first year, as well as his basic physical potential, are also important in influencing later feeding behaviour. Controlled experiments with small mammals show that feeding patterns established in the first few weeks of life persist to affect the rate of growth and life span. In the human infant the maternal attitudes which arose in the pregnancy may survive and become compounded as the mother takes on the task of caring for her baby as a separate but still dependent being. Feeding difficulties may be the rule or may occur at some point during the first year. Until recently, society, including doctors, encouraged robust weight-gain in babies as a sign of vigour and health. Now it is realized that over-feeding may be a disservice.

As the child grows, food begins to take on *psychosocial* meanings for him. In the early months it may be his main contact with his mother. When he is distressed, frightened or cold, his mother may attempt to give food to comfort him. At other times he may be ignored. He may learn that he can best provoke his mother's anxiety by refusing to eat. Feeding problems in young children often have such a basis, interwoven with the child's developing physical capacities.

At this stage, the mother, through feelings of guilt that she may not recognize in herself, or because she lacks a wider competence as a mother, may feed excessive amounts to her young child as a substitute for her love and affection. These may be lacking because of her feelings, sometimes unrecognized, of hostility and rejection. Certainly, children are often given food as a solace when they are miserable or angry, and also as a reward when they have been helpful or compliant. Such a child might grow up prizing food more than human relationships and very uncertain of itself in a social context. At the same time many people set great store by food as a source of strength and wellbeing. In some families, food and feeding appear to be the thing that binds them securely together. The nervous, overprotective mother who anxiously nurtures her child in this way so as to "prepare him for the future" demonstrates one aspect of this neurotic behaviour. Such a mother may feel great anxiety over anything her child does outside her direct supervision and yet rarely attend to his differential cues and instead interact only through feeding. The child, needing to establish a balance in life through realistic perception of and differentiation between internal (e.g. hunger) and external (e.g. social) stimulation, may instead find these stimuli over-lapping each other and then have great difficulty in securing a social as distinct from a physical identity.

Given such social forces—food intake during childhood also remains closely linked to the growth process which is programmed very early in life and which will now continue unfettered provided nourishment and security are adequate and disease does not intrude.

Thus the inevitable slowing down of growth in the second and third year is associated with reduced food intake and the acceleration as puberty begins is accompanied by increasing food intake. A few years ago the Food and Nutrition Board of the National Academy of Sciences of the United States published some guidelines concerning energy and protein requirements for all age groups. The portion covering the adolescent period is shown in Table I. The proposed requirements reflect an increase over levels required for basal needs and growth by a

TABLE 1. Recommended daily dietary allowances for naturally developing adolescents.*

	Age (yr)	Weight (kg)	Height (cm)	Energy (kcal)	Protein (g)
Males	11-14	44	158	2800	44
	15-18	61	172	3000	54
Females	11-14	44	155	2400	44
	15-18	54	162	2100	48

*Adapted from Recommended Dietary Allowances, 8th ed., National Sciences, 1974.

factor of 20 to 30% to allow for individual variation above the usual needs. It can be seen that the divergence in timing of puberty and of overall ultimate size between males and females by the age of 15 to 18 years is reflected in a need for substantially less calorie intake in females by this time, bearing in mind that now, as part of her body weight, she is already carrying twice as much fat as her male counterpart. Other factors such as levels of activity are also obviously crucial in determining food intakes during puberty necessary for normal growth.

The surge of appetite in young adolescents is often very obvious. Every young person experiences this emerging and new force along with other new experiences befalling him or her as a result of sexual maturation, and can be seen to wrestle with it. Eating often becomes erratic—parents despair as their children insist firstly on not eating properly at table and then evidently consume large quantities of carbohydrate on the side. The adolescent's behaviour at this time may reflect his wider clash with his family but also his or her personal battle over impulse control and the need to secure a sense of self and of self-esteem.

It is in this arena, when eating becomes particularly equated with emerging sexuality through its symbolic link, its biological primacy over the latter, the intervening factor of biological maturity as reflected in shape, and the implications of these for the individual and her family that, in my opinion, the seeds of anorexia nervosa root. However, to attempt a fuller understanding one must also examine the complex existential and social implications of biological maturity and especially sexuality for the person and family concerned, and it is within this latter context that each case of anorexia nervosa takes on its uniqueness. These aspects will be explored in succeeding chapters. Meanwhile it is now timely to revert to examining whether, within childhood, there is anything known that characterizes the anorectic-to-be in respect of eating and social patterns.

In Anorexia Nervosa

People's memories and reports of past experience, especially those things most important to them, may sometimes be very distorted and patchy. Information concerning childhood experiences gleaned from anorectics and their families many years later must therefore be viewed with caution. However, many such families, in treatment, strive to be as accurate in their recollections as possible, and there are certain themes that emerge and which appear to be relevant. Once again they are not always present and they are several, revealing the ubiquitous nature of the disorder.

It appears to me that the importance of childhood experience for both the anorectic and her family is that it often in no way equips them to cope with the thrust and demands of puberty. Many anorectic's parents will say such things as "She was the last person we thought would ever develop anorexia nervosa"; "She seemed so effective and confident as a child"; "She was such a good child"; "She was always emphatic that she didn't want to grow up, she was like a Peter Pan"; "Yes we love babies"; "Yes we wanted a son but she was such a tomboy, she really seemed to enjoy playing with trains and watching football matches with her father"; "Yes he was so like his father from the start we knew he would grow up to be like him".

We must however remain wary of making the assumption of psycho-analysts, especially of the Kleinian school, who have some profound contributions to make in other respects, that anorexia nervosa can be understood only and entirely when the earliest infant/mother relationship has been clearly dissected out. Such thinking ignores the biological effects of puberty including its own discrete and existential challenge and the major relevance of this for character formation during adolescence. It is rooted in the willingness to accept the symptoms of anorexia nervosa, the superficial and most readily available language of the anorectic and her family, focussed as it is on eating rather than body shape, and the current morbid transactions with the family, as being of primary and exclusive significance so far as aetiology is concerned.

It has already been mentioned that statistically speaking anorectics tend to be the youngest or younger amongst sibling groups. This in itself is probably associated with greater than average appetite. It is common for parents to claim that their anorectic daughter had a good appetite during childhood, though once again not invariably so. Reports of marked food faddiness during childhood are rare. Most investigators, studying large numbers of anorectics, have been impressed with the relative absence of childhood neurotic traits and behaviour problems. Anorectics, as has already been suggested, are often regarded as "good" and "compliant" children. Sometimes the female anorectic has been a tomboy as a child, sharing her father's interests. Parents will sometimes vividly recall their child's reiterated wish never to grow up. The anorectic-to-be can be either the least or the most favoured child of one or both parents, both in the parents' eyes and in her own estimation. She can have been shy and isolated or gregarious and confident as a child. Such patterns are of course the stuff of childhood in general. Their relevance for anorexia nervosa is in the manner in which these factors relate to other strands of development, family crisis and lack of relevant personal resource in the anorectic-to-be once adolescence has been embarked upon. As emphasized before, it is perhaps this unique convergence of processes to reveal a vulnerability which might otherwise remain covert that in my view characterizes anorexia nervosa.

6
Existential Aspects of Maturation

The early development of a sense of childhood's self in terms of existence separate from objects outside the self has been extensively studied by psychologists like Piaget and by psychiatrists, especially those concerned with object relations and separation/individuation theories. The process is clearly governed by basic physiological maturational processes which require facilitation and amplification by the environment. As individual infantile memories consolidate and come to allow effective predictions based on experience to operate so, presumably, a sense of self in time also crystallizes out. Meanwhile the capacity of parents to care for and yet at the same time respect and allow self-expression in their children, to provide continuity of love and ample stimulation, to share honest feelings and affection and generally introduce elements of mutual self-esteem, to *permit* them not only *to live* but *to be* is probably crucial to a developing sense of worth and intact social self. Such responsibilities usually fall upon the family and are governed by the parents' own resources in a psychological and social sense, by their relationship, and by the meaning of the existence of this particular child to each of them. Such factors are also crucial at the time of their offspring's adolescence. Thus it is puberty that intrudes massively into the world of the child and demands that the sense of self enlarge so as to incorporate sexuality and decay in ways adaptive to the available social matrix. This can present an entirely new challenge to the parents. Some parents cope better with their offspring as children, some when they become adolescent.

The Sense of Self in Terms of Body Weight, Volume and Shape

The small world of the foetus is globular. If it is sensed at all, then it is probably through general physiochemical mechanisms which allow the foetus to locate itself optimally within it.

The newborn infant is busy attempting to bond itself to the mother through such reciprocal activities as smiling, clutching and smelling. Another important initial, and probably visually vague, perception is often of the mother's breasts which may themselves provide warmth, food and general comfort, or otherwise be physically close to him whilst he is being "artificially" fed. As his perception of other people's shapes, sometimes present and sometimes absent, and their associated and different meanings for him begins to sharpen, so perhaps does his sense of his own shape and its meaning also develop within the genetic limits set on neuronal maturation.

The majority of children do not seem overly concerned about their shape unless it be strikingly abnormal. Very fat children are, of course, usually teased and may become very self-conscious. They may come to consider that any inadequacies they feel they have are due to their fatness. However, very few children strive to diet. In children there is often a sense of timelessness, and that time is on their side—some time in the future will be soon enough to deal with such problems.

The libido theory of psychoanalysis postulates a latency period between the age of about five years and puberty, when the child appears relatively unengaged in sexual matters. The theory postulates that prior to this the child has been physically very aware of itself and of its parents, culminating in its recognition of its gender sex through the process of a series of forced realignments in its relationships with the mother and father. Certainly the majority of children during the second half of their childhood appear to be relatively unconcerned about sexual matters and about their appearance, although generally aware of the physical differences between themselves and the other sex. Preoccupation with shape and appearance of self and of others comes for the majority with puberty.

Pubertal girls (and their parents) first become aware of their breast development. Such development can, especially if achieved early, become a source of acute embarrassment and, for instance, stops such girls from going swimming or participating in communal sports. Excuses usually take the form of feeling generally unwell, tummy pains, etc. Other girls, of course, welcome their bust development, may feel it is insufficient or may be indifferent to it. There is thus a wide range of responses to this very first change in "fatness" depending on such factors as the actual degree of the change and its meaning to the girl and those around her. *For the first time* food becomes equated with this new dimension of body weight, volume and shape—henceforth anorexia nervosa is part of the repertoire of possible morbid responses to maturational problems.

As already described in Chapter 4, other pubertal changes now follow each other remorselessly. Some girls feel that these things are happening *to* them rather than that such developments are part and parcel of *themselves*. This new existential dimension of passivity may compound previous passivity and dependency feelings of childhood. The individual does not feel autonomous or that she owns her changing body. As hips and thighs become fatter, as previously fat legs thicken, sensitivity and anxiety about the process sometimes increases to high levels. A few years after the onset of puberty the majority of girls in our society today are striving to reduce their "fatness" or some aspect of it. A specific trigger to such concern may be apparent but rarely accounts in itself for the subsequent preoccupation. This latter has a larger meaning. Thus some girls become sensitive when their bust size outstrips that of their mother's, perhaps often initially having anticipated this within a secret ambition; another girl suddenly realizes that her heavy thighs mark her out as destined to grow like her mother and all that that implies; another girl suddenly comes to believe that the pad of fat at the front of her waist makes her look pregnant. Many girls gain the ability to diet successfully because they share this wish with their girlfriends. Competitiveness, an aim of becoming more "attractive" than before or than one's girlfriend can reinforce such behaviour.

By the age of 17 or 18 years, 70% or more of girls, whether studied in Scandinavia, the United Kingdom or North America, are not only concerned about their "fatness" but also about "dieting" in some way or other. In many of them body shape is beginning to fluctuate in a marked way. In the experimental laboratory situation it has now been shown, as inferred in Chapter 3, that many teenage girls grossly over-estimate their body width or at least report this quality to others—a property that distinguishes them from older normal weight females and from the majority of males. It is a moot point as to whether such behaviour has characterized our society in the past. In the past, of course, food has often been in short supply; many people including adolescents have been undernourished either with or without chronic infection. In times past fashions have sometimes reflected a widespread concern amongst grown women to appear as if they have more female body fat than is the case. False breasts and buttocks (the latter in the form of bustles) have been popular (Figs 11–14).

Nevertheless I suspect that the preoccupation with normal pubertal

FIG. 11. The sculptured image of an ancient Mediterranean fertility goddess, highlighting the fatness of thighs.

"fatness" has been present in society in the past, perhaps not so common and perhaps more prevalent during certain epochs than others. What characterizes our present times? This will be examined in more detail later in this chapter. Meanwhile, I believe that such present widespread attempts of normal weight adolescent girls to reduce their fatness is a profound statement concerning the present nature of our society and the problems it has concerning restraint and impulse control. Such dieting, consciously aimed at promoting attractiveness, in the event fosters powerful internal control mechanisms necessary to many developing adolescents, who enter a society bereft of structure or much in the way of agreed behaviour guidelines and codes of conduct. This social uncertainty is coupled with present day society's questioning of the inevitability of biological destiny, especially that of the female, whilst at the same time inviting her to become "liberated". Curbing shape and fatness for the newly adult female becomes a process directly central and symbolically relevant to her adolescence, not least in terms of her increasing need to control her newfound sexuality. Such links do not naturally exist within the male.

A PIG in a POKE

FIG. 12. The eighteenth century pre-occupation with social images of desirable female fatness and sexuality. Reproduced by courtesy of the Trustees of the British Museum.

The term "dysmorphophobia" has been coined to describe disorders, usually arising during adolescence, wherein the individual becomes acutely sensitive about some aspect of shape and indeed phobic or fearful of it. This book is concerned with anorexia nervosa. Female "fatness" of one form or another has been focussed on. However, both males and females can also become very sensitive about other aspects of their bodies; the shape of their noses or the size and position of their ears for instance. From my clinical experience, such burgeoning preoccupation in adolescence is often rooted in other aspects of the adolescent identity crisis. Although sometimes related symbolically to some aspect of sexual development, it may also reflect more basic mechanisms such as a rejection of identification, biologically and/or socially driven, with one or other parent or other family members who shares the same physical characteristic. Such mechanisms are often vigorously denied by the individual concerned when examined within a superficial encounter.

NORMAL   LOW
CARBOHYDRATE   CARBOHYDRATE

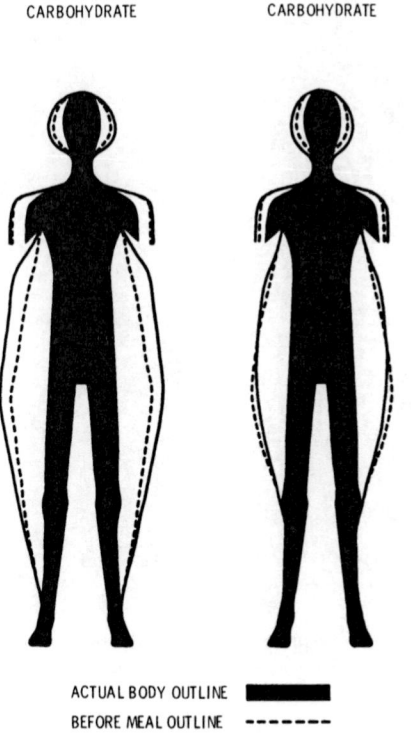

ACTUAL BODY OUTLINE   ■■■■■■
BEFORE MEAL OUTLINE   - - - - - - - -
AFTER MEAL OUTLINE   ───────

FIG. 13. Diagrammatic representation of an anorectic's reported estimates of her body width, which characteristically reflect a gross over-estimation. It can be seen that these are further inflated following the ingestion of carbohydrate as distinct from fat and protein containing similar amounts of calories. This does not normally happen, and reflects the anorectic's special and distorted view of carbohydrate.

Other adolescents retain a poorly developed sense of their own bodies and have great difficulty tuning into them. I believe that excessive masturbation, sadism and masochism, and self-mutilation are often driven by desperate attempts by the individuals concerned to get in touch with their own bodies and to "feel alive".

Intense anxiety in itself is associated with states called "depersonalization" and "derealization", wherein one's own body and the outside world respectively feel unreal to the individual concerned. Such experiences seem to be part of the direct physiological expression of an intense anxiety along with the urge to flee and a general state of autonomic arousal. Only a marginal or *borderline* sense of the self exists and this is predominantly in terms of shape.

So what of the male and his shape concerns? Certainly very few males become deeply sensitive about their fatness. Those who do are either very fat and therefore reasonably and healthily sensitive, or are characterized by profound doubts about their gender identity, or else essentially

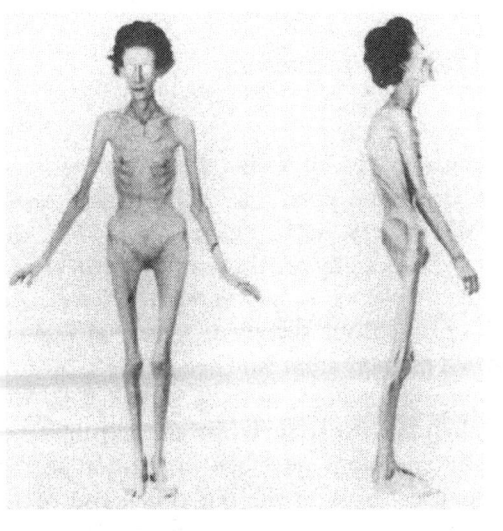

FIG. 14. A photograph of an emaciated anorectic who nevertheless felt herself to be always in imminent danger of becoming like the shapes outlined in Figs. 11 and 13.

experience themselves as female. It is out of this population of adolescent males sensitized for one reason or another either to their massive obesity or the sexual implications of their shape, that a small minority go on to develop anorexia nervosa, given also the other operative forces that help to generate this condition.

Many males are more interested in actually increasing their lean body mass, physical strength and strong appearance. They are much less likely to curb their natural appetite than females. Some, especially the more insecure, whatever their size and shape, may become preoccupied with body-building and excessively with physical fitness. Genital size may become a preoccupation. Small genitalia may become a source of shame. Large genitalia may become a focus of pride, envy or guilt, e.g. in comparison with father, and in a sexually intimate family in which rivalry for the mother's attention going back into childhood has been or is potentially being rekindled, at least at the fantasy level, by the advent of puberty.

The present emphasis that adolescents place on their shape and size is, I suggest, importantly related to the nature of our society, its value systems and the conflicting messages that we as parents deliver. The next section concerns the wider issue of identity formation, of which self-awareness of shape is just a part.

Overall Identity Formation

Identity formation, a frustrating concept, or rather a number of over-lapping and sometimes conflicting concepts, has preoccupied many philosophers, poets, priests and others over the centuries. For the present-day clinician, and perhaps especially for those involved in trying to help adolescents in distress, it seems a real enough process. An individual's sense of self and worth in our society is, partly at least, a socially and psychologically based phenomenon, and becomes established in relation to the social and cultural context, initially provided by the family and its value systems, beliefs and capacity to care and nurture.

Although it is socio-culturally shaped it develops in relation to the underlying and operative biological forces in the individual and social system. These are fundamentally different in childhood, in adult reproductive life and in adult post-reproductive life.

In childhood the experience of biological maturity exists only at the imaginative level, rooted in observing parents and other adults, not least these days via our channels of mass and immediate communication and stimulation such as television. The experience cannot be personally relevant at this stage except as something to be anticipated at some indeterminate point in the future, perhaps pleasurably, fearfully or indifferently. This will be true for the child and for those involved with him or her and contemplating his or her development and its implications for themselves.

As puberty triggers the reality of this confrontation it becomes neces-sary for everyone concerned to cope with the emergent new biological drives and their social consequences. At the same time the individual and those around them retain the memory of their own childhood experience and identity, as they were and as they now construe themselves or are now construed as having been.

Following midlife and personal biological involution around the sixth decade of existence, a new confrontation arises which once again challenges identity not only in relation to the biological processes at work but also to their social implications and concomitant social processes, such as confrontation with the actual limits of achievement, the experience of mounting personal losses, disengagement of one's own children and closer confrontation with the inevitability of personal decay and death. Each stage will affect the individual's identity, achievements and capacity to cope within the next phase.

This section attempts to offer a schema of the processes which appear to be formative in the initial establishment of adult identity. No one schema seems to be ideal and, as has previously been stated, they are inevitably culture-bound. Personal identity is a very different matter in Buddhist or Taoist Asia than in the western world. The western world is clearly not a single entity in cultural terms. The old Christian cultures are fundamentally different between themselves. Catholic versus Puritan-based culture for instance; and both these are totally different from Jewish-based culture. Much of the psychoanalytic writing on this subject is by Jewish authors involved to a greater or lesser extent in non-Jewish cultures. It is easy enough to understand how many Jewish people come to be engaged in this topic of identity formation. Like many others, I am indebted in particular to Eric Ericson; in his writings over the last few decades he has managed to convey a sense of the ingredients of the normal adolescent maturational process which rings true and which provides many a peg on which to hang one's own thinking, clinical experience and therapeutic endeavours, not to mention one's own personal experiences. He has defined a sense of identity as "a feeling of being at home in one's body, a sense of knowing where one is going, and an inner assurance of anticipated recognition from those who count".

The process leading to this formation is only made possible once some degree of effective separation has been achieved by the adolescent within the "dependence/independence conflict" which precedes it and blends with it.

The formation of identity requires the integration of the new biological sexuality within oneself both with one's basic social needs, sense of self-esteem and competence and one's set of values. This process often, and healthily so, takes several years. During this, the individual casts off or inspects in a new detached way what may be experienced as previously

personal development. For attempts at explanation of this, one perhaps needs to penetrate to whether those robust childhood social resources are relevant to the tasks of adolescence on the one hand and whether the environment, especially including the family, is going to mobilize them to this task on the other hand. For instance, it is going to be difficult for a child brought up with one set of gender expectations to incorporate another set imposed by puberty. It is going to be difficult for a child whose present role is crucial to the family or to one parent's personal integrity to cope with the social and personal disruption among them that attempted adolescent maturation will provoke.

The Social Matrix

A hundred and fifty years ago, in our western society, adolescence barely existed. Transition from childhood to adulthood in terms of social role was not as instantaneous as in so-called primitive cultures, but actually involved overlap. Prepubertal children were obliged to work and denied education. Only as society became more complicated did the concept of adolescence emerge. Gradually separate judicial systems arose in relation to children and adults, implicitly recognizing the existence of a transitional period between these two states. Children and young adolescents were increasingly forbidden to work for a living and obliged instead to study. Within society the length of the newfound phase called adolescence, the latter part of it being elective, began to vary according to family social backgrounds and value systems. Until recently this period, involving continued dependence at least in material terms upon the family, carried with it increasingly complex ground rules. Compliance and constraint within the family were buttressed by society through, for instance, authoritarian legislation, and courtship rituals.

The social matrix, so structured in the recent past, is now much less so, thereby demanding greater structure *within* the self in the face of such freedom and lack of guidelines. It has perhaps been the rejection and dismantling of such social structures that has given birth to the existential philosophies with their preoccupation with *isolation* and *alienation* and their rejection of psychic dualism. (Psychic dualism has been touched on in Chapter 1.)

In addition and against the background of extraordinary and increasingly rapid scientific and technological developments over the last few centuries, social historians claim to detect an underlying cycle of restraint and permissiveness in social life. The Protestant movement of the late 16th and early 17th centuries, embodying concepts of subservience to God, hard work, thrift, soberness and sexual restraint, gave way to an increasing permissiveness in the next hundred years, culminating in George III's proclamation against vice in 1789. He closed brothels and gambling houses and suppressed "all loose and licentious prints, books and publications".

This development crystallized out as a predominantly middle class drive for the moral regeneration of the poor (and hence perhaps themselves), on the basis that sexual constraint was now firmly established as a cornerstone of middle class value systems; and it survived as a social force for the next century at least. Since then it has slowly given way or perhaps fragmented until the last 20 years, when entirely new forces appear to have taken over.

Meanwhile, such moral attitudes during periods of restraint were mirrored in the system within the family which was essentially patriarchal and restrictive. Doubtless there were always independent or dissonant attitudes co-existing with such cycles but it is claimed that they were insignificant. In the past 80 years, however, the situation has grown more complex. The population has greatly increased. The countryside has become largely denuded of population—the final consequence of the Industrial Revolution reaching out into it. Geographical mobility has increased dramatically again, and on a much larger scale. Industry and government have become increasingly centralized and impersonal. The State, with its protective legislation, has taken over responsibility for the care not only of the sick but also the handicapped and underprivileged. The feminist movement for social equalization of women has gained momentum. Leisure time has become a reality. Along with all of this has come adequate nutrition for all and increasingly effective preventive medicine, ensuring optimal physical growth and well-being. At the same time institutions and ritual are in disarray and at bay. The influence of Christianity as a dogmatic statement has waned to the point of extinction. There are no longer any clear-cut rules or limits on behaviour for the emerging adult to accept unquestioningly. In the last 20 years two most important factors have been the development of female contraceptive techniques which have fundamentally altered the nature of sexual relationships, especially outside marriage, and also the development of mass media and instant communication. Children and young adults are exposed to a welter of information, much of it commercially motivated, which is immediately attractive and which at the same time reveals to them the true needs of the majority of their parents who obviously subscribe to it. Society in general is often seen to be impulse-ridden and materialistic, and the young feel more free to disregard parental value systems.

There are probably always social factors, both historical and immediate, that can be usefully construed as relevant to the anorectic's stance. They are rooted in the above forces and reflect predominantly either the incipient anorectic's simple incapacity to cope with the challenges presented, or else the implicit demand to "conform or else" required of her by her immediate environment and attachments in the face of these same challenges to it. In the present climate it is so-called middle class value systems, especially those centring on sexual conduct, that are most out of step with society at large, whether they be adopted by professional or working class families. This factor probably contributes to the increased prevalence of the condition, at least until very recently, within middle class families. There are of course many other contexts within which the family can still be seen as part of a larger system and where a culture clash is inevitable because of the rigidity of the system in question. In my view this accounts for the high incidence and prevalence of the condition amongst certain strict religious sects in this country and was, for instance, an important factor in the cause of anorexia nervosa in a young Arab girl I saw recently, confronted by the enormity of the gap between her village Islamic tradition and family mores on the one hand, the bewildering experience and immediate attractiveness of Western influences on the other, and the need to "choose" in the face of an unbending conservative parental attitude.

At this stage it is important to remember, however, that other factors, including not least an impulse to behave in exactly the opposite way to that characterizing the conformity of anorexia nervosa are necessary to the condition. Some of these will be discussed in the next chapter.

7
The Maturational Crisis in Anorexia Nervosa

In my view the onset of anorexia nervosa is preceded by a social maturational crisis which the subsequent illness serves to resolve. Two aspects of this crisis will be considered here. Firstly, the crisis as perceived within the individual herself, and secondly the crisis as it arises within the family. There is no antithesis intended, for, whilst each individual contributes purely personal factors to it, the central ingredient is that which is common to them all.

The Crisis Viewed in the Adolescent's Terms

People do not always give full or accurate reasons for their behaviour. Their explanations are governed by their self-understanding and by the image they wish to present. If teenage girls are asked in a survey why they are dieting they are likely to say such things as "I want to lose weight", "I want to be more attractive", "My friends were dieting and I joined them", "Because my mother was dieting", and so on. Such responses merely invite further questions, e.g. Is it weight or shape that you want to change? If shape, then which aspect of your shape and why? Attractive to whom? Why are your friends dieting? and so on. The answers to such questions are less easy to come by and we do not know what their form and frequency is. It is therefore not possible to say whether the initial motivation of the anorectic-to-be, when she starts to diet, is either quantitatively or even qualitatively different from that of the average teenager. In my view it is not, and the picture being presented here is of dieting behaviour—usually carbohydrate avoidance—becoming amplified (overdetermined to use a psychoanalytic concept, rewarded to use a behavioural one) for *other* reasons.

In my work with anorectic patients and their families I have come across a number of themes, some of which I will attempt to illustrate. Although they inevitably stem from specific cases they have been changed so that characters cannot be recognised and often they represent a condensation of information from a number of cases. Sometimes such psychopathology is self-evident; at other times it is masked by denial and will only be yielded under highly specific conditions.

Family Constellations Associated with an Anorectic Child

1. The Adolescent Child's Challenge to the Identity of the Parents and to their Relationship

It has been suggested that it is natural for our adolescent children to challenge our own adjustments. Indeed sometimes the challenge is so specific that it demands some fresh personal growth of a major kind in ourselves for us to cope with it other than by suppression or rejection of our offspring. Yet the price of such change may also be threatening. By middle life we have largely and conveniently forgotten the struggles and turmoil of our own adolescence. Our lifestyle has long crystallized out, determining our occupation, our handwriting, our value systems and our marriages. Unless such adjustments are relatively secure and healthy, they may need to be even more soundly defended than before in the face of an adolescent offspring who rekindles our old uncertainties. Let us take two relatively complex examples:

A. Mr and Mrs Brown had been married for 24 years. Jennifer, now with anorexia nervosa, is their youngest child. Both Mr and Mrs Brown are inwardly aware of the fragile and hence necessarily rigid nature of their relationship and personal adjustment. Mr Brown, now alternatively impulsive and indecisive in nature, still prone to occasional gambling and with a rarely talked-about phase of his early life in which, rebelling against his strict family background, he drank heavily for a while and got into trouble with the police, is married to his stern, conscientious and dominant wife. Mrs Brown had suffered severe indigestion and had been investigated for gastric pathology 17 years previously, but had recovered coincidentally with the enforced cessation of an affair her husband was having with a female colleague at his office. Subsequently Mr Brown had become depressed for a while and shortly after this Jennifer had been conceived. Mutual wariness and grimness actually characterized their relationship, although to their friends they seemed to have a reassuringly stable life. In fact, within it, they both found a necessary sense of containment and identity. Jennifer was her mother's favourite until puberty, when another side of the daughter's nature, more allied to that of her father, began to show itself. She had become rebellious, sullen and secretive, hanging around with boys her mother disapproved of, sensitive about her appearance, and dieting sporadically. Indeed there were times, especially in the first few months, when Jennifer sensed that her father secretly approved of her new behaviour. Now her mother increasingly rejected her, showing more interest instead in her charitable works and her young grandchildren. Rows between her parents escalated. Mr Brown found himself blamed for Jennifer's behaviour and in turn became critical and dismissive of her. Despite her blustering, Jennifer felt increasingly insecure and desperate. Another phase of dieting this time rapidly escalated, she lost weight and her menstrual bleeding ceased early on. She lost interest in boys and they in her. Her parents were now seemingly more united than ever in their common concern for her, although Mrs Brown never grasped that Jennifer's real reason for not eating was so that she could maintain her body weight below about 40 kgs. Indeed Mrs Brown became increasingly distressed that she could not enable Jennifer to eat and felt in some way deeply responsible. However she did realize that, once again, Jennifer was like her in her nature. Indeed as the years went by the two of them became convinced that they had a special understanding of each other to the point of mutual telepathic powers.

B. Mr Baker was a very wealthy businessman. He produced sweets, and it could be said that he owed his success, indeed his entire lifelong preoccupation with his job, to his chronic anorexia nervosa. Despite his "illness", more or less effectively disguised from the world because of his male clothing and people's acceptance, albeit sometimes with mild surprise, of his skinny appearance, restrained eating habits and associated tightly controlled social routine, he had married. Mrs Baker was a very attractive and well-preserved lady, both of them now in their mid-forties. Their marriage was unconsummated and indeed they could both be seen, if value judgements are allowed, as having entirely failed to cope effectively with the sexuality emergent in their youth. Nevertheless they were in certain ways caring people and keen to adopt a child. This they achieved. Inevitably Rosalind was an illegitimate child and she was lusty and a fast developer in a physical sense. During her childhood the family life was idyllic. They were very proud of her and lavished care upon her; especially she was well nourished. Perhaps they were particularly proud of their ability to cope with this situation. But as Rosalind passed through puberty, somewhat plump, she began to look and behave increasingly like her mother whom they had both once met. Her tentative early forays into the world of coffee shops and boyfriends in the nearby town were too much for them to bear. Her adoptive mother, projecting her own lifelong imagination into these excursions, was reduced to screaming at her "You're just like your mother—a tart". But Rosalind was deeply attached to her adoptive parents, she truly cared for them and was grateful to them for their love of her. She had no other home or people to which and to whom she belonged. Struggling as she had been to assert herself, by making her appearance slightly more trim—a step which had merely intensified the family anxieties—she slipped rapidly into anorexia nervosa, and once again became compliant and restricted to the home. This adoptive family's problems were now different and the nature of the initial turmoil was deleted as the "illness" became the only focus of concern now necessary.

2. The Pan-phobic Household

Mr and Mrs Green were not dissimilar in their makeup from Mr and Mrs Brown. However, Mr Green was extraordinarily meek and inoffensive. They had no friends outside the close family, and rarely went out except to the shops and to have their annual holiday, always then in a tight family group. Mrs Green, although seemingly strong-willed and dominant eventually admitted that she became panicky when out alone, especially in strange places, and could see that much of her apparent dominance was in fact rooted in a desperate need always to exercise control over her circumstances. Family life centred around the meal table. There, Mrs Green, obese and motherly, held sway. She was devoted to children and, when a hysterectomy prevented her having more, she began to foster other people's babies. As each child entered adolescence a major crisis arose. Initially her eldest son was clearly her close favourite. He remained apparently bound intimately to her until he reached the age of 18 years, when he suddenly announced that he was leaving home and going to live with a girl of about his own age. Mrs Green had always felt disgusted by sexual matters. She refused ever to visit or talk with or about her son again, and instead began to lavish her affection on Anne, who was at that time aged 14 years. Anne had always felt second best and she responded immediately to her mother's attentions. A year or so later, however, Anne found that her social horizons began to expand and she met some boys, but in her turn she was jeopardizing her newfound relationship with her mother. Unsure of herself sexually she was unable to share her uncertainties with her mother, who was evidently unable to discuss such matters. Indeed Mrs Green had not even been able to discuss the experience of Anne's menarche with her, and no one had ever asked Anne how she felt about it. Now, unable to cope with this and her mother's increasing commitment to a newly fostered baby, she lapsed quickly into anorexia nervosa. She had indeed been sensitive about the size of her bust and waist for several years—they seemed to upset her mother from time to time—and they also reminded Anne of her likeness to her mother and the implications of this for her in years to come. She had been struggling to diet but only now did the process begin to take her over.

In order to understand this case further we need of course to examine the origins of Mrs Green's phobic avoidance behaviour, and the way in which this and her powerful maternal role had protected her from her own sexuality for so many years. We don't need to look far to speculate as to why Anne at the age of 15 had no real personal resources to carry her through the crisis confronting her. She had been raised to be a child, and an unfavoured one at that, and it is not surprising that, as adolescence threatened her she "chose", through her anorexia nervosa, to rejoin her father and younger brothers, sisters and foster siblings as a dependent member of the household.

3. The Family that Never Was

Many marriages now end in separation and divorce. Some, because the partners have truly grown away from each other or, more sadly, one of them has changed and the other not. Some marriages should clearly never have been contrived in the first instance. Mrs Smith was aged 26 and had been married for three years when she first realized that her husband was dissatisfied with their relationship. Although she never knew of the affair he was engaged in she sensed that shortly their marriage would break up. Secretly she stopped taking the Pill and within two months she was pregnant. Her judgement was right. Her husband recommitted himself to the obligations of his marriage. Even before Angela was born Mrs Smith was calculating how old she and her husband would be when their daughter was likely to be showing signs of independence. From the beginning Angela was entwined within their problem. For Mrs Smith she was a precious asset. Mrs Smith was loving and thoughtful by nature, but she dreaded Angela growing up. Mr Smith was a devoted father in many ways—indeed his mere presence now in the family implied his sense of responsibility towards Angela. However, he sometimes appeared impatient with her. Angela grew to be like her mother in appearance and manner, and sometimes felt very close to her father. She worked hard at school but was panicky before exams especially A levels. She did less well than expected and went to study at the local technical college instead of going away to university. During the next year her mother became increasingly depressed and only then did Angela notice that her father was often not at home. He had become deeply involved with a young female colleague at the school at which he taught. Now she contemplated for the first time the significance of the remark she had heard him scream at her mother ten years earlier "You wait till Angela is 18". Angela had never been very confident and had early on decided that this was because she had fat legs like her mother. Within the context of her mounting panic at the prospect of her parents' marriage breaking up her dieting quickly escalated, seeming suddenly easy and relieving to her, and, as anorexia nervosa supervened, her father and mother were reunited in their unwritten contract together to care for her until she "grew up".

It can be seen how Angela's maturational crisis was also her mother's. Angela's panic over 'A' levels was mirroring her mother's unspoken but communicated fears concerning the implications for them all of Angela passing out with adequate grades and then moving away from home. As in all cases of "examination phobia" that I have come across, the precise precipitation by the examination seems only to be usefully understood in terms of its meaning for the individual. The next illustration provides another and different example of the O and A level issue, which by some writers has been elevated to the status of being *the* cause of anorexia nervosa.

4. A Father's Search for Self-fulfillment

Phillipa's father was a doctor. Coming from humble origins and never regarded as the brightest amongst his exceptionally able brothers and sisters, he had nevertheless succeeded more than them in many ways. Very conscientious and caring, apparently benign but essentially dictatorial, he had great faith in the reductionist biochemical approach within medicine and he greatly distrusted psychiatrists and suchlike people, though he always strove to be polite within the present clinical situation. He had always been an introverted man, absorbed by his hobbies of walking and bird-watching. There was a suggestion that he had a phase of anorexia nervosa in his teens, and he remained deeply committed to physical fitness. Mrs Edwards loved and respected her husband deeply and bore him three children. Of them all, Phillipa was the apple of his eye. Academically brilliant, sweet-natured like her artistically talented mother, she applied herself single-mindedly to her work and she was very close to her father. She often went walking with her father. She was not aware that her name stemmed from a last-minute reconstruction of the name Philip which they had chosen for the son they had expected and hoped for. Since the age of 16 she had had anorexia nervosa, and it was a great sadness to him to see her so ill yet he was intensely proud of her sole intention to study medicine and become a doctor. It never occurred to Dr Edwards that anorexia nervosa was the price being paid for her continued excellence, especially the success in her O levels. He had never once been able to invite Phillipa to share her own needs and feelings with him. Thus, since the entire household was committed for one reason or another to protecting him from the realities of adolescence, including undoubtedly his own, he was never aware that for a while she had begun to falter, around the age of 15, before putting such other temptations behind her within the context of her burgeoning anorexia nervosa. For a few months only she had turned her attention partly to other things—to boys and to a concern about her shape—amidst a sense of reality coupled with deep insecurity.

Although she dutifully passed her A levels with flying colours she was very panicky in the run-up to them. Could she do well enough was the question hanging over her—and subsequently, could she cope with the necessity of leaving home for medical school. It was these issues, now still hanging over her despite her anorexia nervosa, that she and her family focussed on in their personal attempts to understand the nature of her illness and before the more complex issues alluded to above became central.

5. Why Should I want to Know Anything About my Father?

Corinne was 26 years old, married for four years to her patient, attentive husband, and she had had severe anorexia nervosa for about five years—in fact since they had got to know each other "well". Mr White never pressed Corinne to talk of her early life, although he knew that she had never known her father and that her sister was in many ways opposite in nature to her. Mrs White was well aware that her husband did not know her "true" nature and saw the link between her present self and her anorexia nervosa on the one hand and her other self—similar in many ways to that of her sister in nature—which would be quite incompatible with her continued marriage to Mr White. It irritated her greatly that he unwittingly and constantly strove to "help" her gain weight. Both of them were in touch with her uncle who, together with her aunt, had brought both the sisters up within their very religious strict evangelical household. It was through them that Mrs White had gleaned some patchy knowledge about her real parents. Her mother, her aunt's sister, was sketched in as an impulsive feckless person now living in a common law relationship with an alcoholic man somewhere in the Midlands. Corinne's father was said to have been a member of the Polish armed forces and to have had only a fleeting relationship with her mother—rendering her pregnant before departing. Occasionally it had been darkly hinted that both the daughters were especially like him in their temperament. Corinne's sister had been rebellious from the start and had been finally ousted from the aunt's home at the age of 17, when, apart from a phase of about nine months, she had been a constant source of distress to the aunt who saw her to be beyond salvation. Corinne, more dependent than her sister and more attached to her aunt, had led a restrained existence until the age of 18, working as a waitress in the local town teashop and seldom going out except to occasional Old Tyme dances. It was there that she had met her husband-to-be. She initially found him dull and was offhand with him. Their early relationship appeared to give her some new assertiveness and she had a brief intense relationship with an older, seductive and dominating man. Somewhat plump, she began to diet. At this stage her aunt died of a myocardial infarction; smitten with remorse, Corinne rapidly lapsed into anorexia nervosa, and settled down to a relationship with her husband-to-be.

Corinne's illness can be seen as a rejection of her true nature, of her real father's and mother's natures, and as the adoption of a lifestyle approved of by her aunt. The crude splitting of people within the family into "good" and "bad" extended, in Corinne's case, literally into splitting off that aspect of herself seen by her aunt as bad.

Her present stance can be viewed as an aspect of her unresolved response to the loss of her aunt, including her secret conviction that she had contributed to the latter's death by her "bad" ways. It could also be seen as securing her marital relationship which, although in many ways unrewarding for her, also provided her with an improbable source of support and security. A man who marries a woman with anorexia nervosa can only be seen as having rather limited needs. It is likely that she will be preoccupied with feeding him up. It is most likely that their sexual relationship, if ever established, as was the case here, will have ceased many years previously.

At her first visit to the clinic Corinne said desperately "Why should I want to know anything about my father—I don't know him". Such a statement, reflecting her wishes, could only hold any meaning so long as she had anorexia nervosa.

6. Anorexia Nervosa in a Young Man

Peter was 18 years old, and had had anorexia nervosa since the age of 14. His father, Mr Winters, had been agoraphobic since adolescence, and, in recent years had been unable even to get to work, becoming instead totally housebound except when going out with the family. A brief phase of impetuosity in the father's youth was now part of the family folklore. Mrs Winters was short of stature. She was a vigorous extrovert person and she had evidently become impatient with her husband's crippling social disability as Peter, her youngest child had begun four or five years before to show some evidence of independence, thereby reducing her day-to-day obligations within the home. She had learnt to drive a car and was planning her first independent holiday.

Peter had shown an increasing mixture of impetuosity and panic avoidance behaviour as he had approached puberty. Bereft of example within his family he had found it difficult to know how to behave. Deeply dependent on his mother, much of the time he felt very unsure of himself and passive in relation to others. One day his mother commented on the size of his genitalia "You're getting as big as your father" she said. This instance, symbolizing as it did the inadequacy of his father and the intensity of Peter's own attachment to his mother, made him acutely aware of his overall size in relation to his father. His one close relationship with another boy took on a sexual aspect and at the same time he was being teased by other boys who sensed his passivity and sensitivity and who found, in his mild obesity, something which which they could taunt him. Put on a strict diet by his father, he at last began to feel some sense of control and purpose coming into his life, and as anorexia nervosa supervened, with all its biologically regressive forces, he experienced increasing relief as his newly simplified existence came to defuse his many emergent problems. Even less equipped to deal with life than was his father, who had coped merely by social avoidance mechanisms, Peter had only anorexia nervosa to fall back on. The "illness" persisted and his parents were more united than before by their concern for him.

7. Like Mother, Like Child—Adolescence Revisited

Pauline was terrified of the new things that seemed to be happening to her, breasts were developing and her thighs were changing shape. People no longer treated her in quite the same way as before. Her mother seemed to have become more withdrawn. Mrs Davies on her part wondered fearfully and guiltily how to deal with Pauline during the coming months. She had told Pauline as much as she could about menstruation, especially the demands it made on cleanliness, and she was waiting to be told that Pauline's first menstrual bleed was happening. Pauline had had a nose bleed and a short while previously had also experienced some abdominal pain which both she and Mrs Davies independently and unbeknown to each other had concluded was probably a preamble to such a menstrual bleed. Mrs Davies recalled to herself as best she could her own early teens. She remembered the overriding feeling that something was happening to her body that was beyond her control. She remembered her own tummy pains and the appendectomy that had followed, fluctuations in her weight, the years of periodic secret eating and vomiting. She knew that it was within this context that she had married Mr Davies, also at a time when her mother had recently died. She remembered the phase of determined dieting that had developed on the day of their marriage, the long weeks of non-consummation of their relationship, the ultimate conception and her shame at her pregnancy, and her success at concealing it by vomiting and keeping her weight down for so many months. Still no one suspected that she had the seeds of anorexia nervosa within her. After Pauline's birth she had determined once and for all to get her weight down and banish her dreadful fatness. During the pregnancy she had become constipated and had begun to purge herself. She felt marvellous after having her bowels open, her tummy felt flat and the flesh on her face felt more taut. For the past 12 years she had secretly taken 15 sennacot tablets daily. She had had many investigations for her tummy pain, chronic diarrhoea and bouts of weakness, and also her near-emaciated state. A diagnosis of mild but intractable ulcerative colitis had been made on more than one occasion. In her marriage she was dutiful and houseproud. There had been no sexual relationship in the marriage since shortly after Pauline's birth, when their single attempt had left her sobbing and shrieking out to be left alone. She remembered guiltily that Pauline as a baby had been sleeping in their bedroom at the time. Her restlessness especially at night had been the reason they had both focussed on as justifying them beginning to sleep in separate rooms about 10 years ago. Life had been a great struggle for Mrs Davies but she felt that she had done her best. She still sensed sometimes that her mother was watching her and might even approve of her efforts one day; but now she was confronted by these changes in Pauline and she did not know how to respond. She knew deep down that she was to blame for her daughter's present anxieties. Pauline had always been a strange mixture as a child. Initially enthusiastic and pressing in her desire to go off with friends for the day or to camp for a few days, she would shortly after panic and refuse to budge. Mrs Davies had tried to conceal the relief she had often felt when this happened. Then a few weeks ago she had seen a bunch of boys following Pauline home from school. She sensed that Pauline was both fascinated and frightened by this attention, but she had been unable to talk with her about it. She was certainly going to insist on Saturday that Pauline bought a longer skirt, and she must remember to check on whether Pauline's bowels were working properly. Her husband sometimes appeared to deliberately thwart her in her attempts to discipline Pauline these days. Getting cross with Pauline only seemed to intensify the sense of helplessness she had about her contribution as a mother.

As Pauline began to get thinner the imminent prospect of her having her first menstrual bleed seemed to Mrs Davies to lessen also. Pauline was now staying in her room a great deal of the time when she was at home, and had in fact begun to prefer to eat her meals there. The teddy bear to which she had always remained attached seemed to have become again of central importance to her. She carried it everywhere and was sleeping with it again. Mrs Davies got a sense of relief from the obvious innocence of this relationship. In their separate worlds both Mr and Mrs Davies had the same complex experiences of relief and guilt at the same time. Occasionally Mr Davies found himself thinking bitterly about his mother, and his image of himself as a child, screaming and striking out, would come into his mind. At least in his present marriage he felt relief in the absence of demands made upon him by his wife, who at the same time seemed wholly committed to keeping their home spotlessly clean and to cooking meals for him. Mrs Davies hurried out to buy another large carton of purgatives, making sure that she avoided the chemist's shop which had provided her with a similar purchase just a few days before. Pauline was shortly going to need some of her supply.

SECTION III

The Mechanisms and Processes within Anorexia Nervosa

8
An Attempted Explanation of the Immediate Experiential and hence also the Behavioural and Physical Features of the Condition

This chapter and the next are an attempt to explain some of the immediate features of anorexia nervosa, previously described in detail in Chapter 2. We are in an age when teleology is often frowned upon, but to the clinical biologist there may be a certain attraction in searching for purposive and causal linkages. There is fascination in the detective process involved in such a search and, for those in the caring professions, there is the aim of thereby discovering effective means of intervention and treatment. The hazards of the approach include a propensity to project one's own expectations and search for personal solutions in life onto the sought-after explanatory processes. The following attempts at explanations are therefore offered within this acknowledged context.

It must be restated that others have viewed the disorder as primarily constitutionally based (i.e. owing nothing or little to current experiential factors and to social adaptive processes and mechanisms), or else have emphasized the primary importance of the current eating disorder for the determination of the condition. In contrast I have always claimed that the primary experiential behavioural determinant of the condition is rooted in adolescent concern, usually female, about body shape, fatness and weight. In this way it is in profound contrast to the common feeding disorders of childhood which so often relate directly to the mother/child interaction. I have never come across an anorectic who, speaking frankly, could say other than that, if she could eat freely or even hugely without gaining weight then this would be not only no problem for her but sometimes also a special delight. Of course many anorectics learn just this skill, through the medically sinister development of vomiting ingested food.

In my view, an understanding of the total condition stems from this point of departure *given* also the presence of constitutional factors (social, behavioural and physical), no one of which is absolutely necessary for the condition.

Also, I believe that the diagnostic term anorexia nervosa is unsatisfactory. If it is to survive then it needs to be buttressed by a recognition that rather than nervous loss of appetite, there is a massive embargo on eating or retaining ingested food because of its implications for weight gain. The initial determination to diet and the progressively intense "pursuit of thinness" (Hilde Bruch's term) crystallizes out as an overwhelming terror and panic of normal adolescent/adult body weight. The fears of fatness and of normal adult body weight are intimately related for reasons that have been elaborated upon earlier, i.e. the latter promotes qualitative biological and psychosocial change in the former within the female pubertal process, and occasionally also, in terms of psychosocial significance, in the male pubertal process and subsequent adolescence.

Anorectics can only contemplate gain of weight up to an immediately sub-pubertal level which is commonly of the order of 6 to 6½ stones (84–91 lbs, 38–41 kgs). Indeed the capacity to maintain a stable weight of this kind would often be seen as ideal by the anorectic. Unfortunately for her such a weight is biologically unstable—she is always in danger of submitting to the basic impulse of the hungry and starving person to eat. It can be argued that at such a weight she is subject to the greatest thrust of all—the immediate threshold of puberty and the natural spurt of growth that heralds it. Thus, only if she is confident of total control over her food intake and hence weight through the mechanism of vomiting may she say to others that truly she does not wish to lose any more weight. In the typical case, however, progressive weight loss below this threshold is an added insurance for her despite the greater immediate physical debility that accompanies these lower body weights. Trapped into the treatment situation, the anorectic's first thought will be to escape without having to gain weight beyond this secondary level of weight variation. I coined the term "adult body *weight phobia*" to encompass the psychopathology at the descriptive level. It emphasizes and identifies for the diagnosis (i) the primary importance of normal adult body weight (and hence shape and fatness), and (ii) the central role of this as the source of the intense panic which also characterizes the condition. The elaborate meaning of adult body weight and fatness in psychosocial terms is, as has been dwelt upon earlier in the book, both complex and not specific to anorexia nervosa. This latter is the third level of diagnosis and also extremely difficult to penetrate, since it is no longer a reality at the time of presentation of the anorectic for help, within her starved state. Thus the disorder, fitting *regressively* around puberty, has embodied the reversal of the pubertal process. It has precipitated the individual and those around her back into the experience of her being a child biologically and hence also in many ways psychologically and socially. All that she and they retain psychologically of her post-pubertal experience and their experience of her as an adolescent, are memories which are no longer relevant to her and to their current interaction, and indeed which may be forgotten or denied. To this extent the condition is a profound *phobic avoidance* process, which can usefully be compared with the less primitive agoraphobic syndrome, within which only *social* avoidance mechanisms prevail.

Instead of these precipitating experiences, now perhaps some years old, being to the fore, the anorectic's current experiential status is fundamentally different, as is that of those around her.

Her mental state and behaviour will be dominated by two forces, (i) her terror of weight gain (her need to maintain her present low body weight or even to lessen it) and hence her ever present need to avoid the personal temptation of eating and avoid the pressure from others upon her to eat. Bereft of other resources she may prefer even to die rather than surrender her present position. (ii) The experiential thrust of her starved state.

It is the ultimate irony for the anorectic that, unlike the starving millions of the world for whom the primacy of hunger is life-saving, she is resisting eating and attempting to starve in the presence of abundant food. Thus it has been shown quite clearly that starvation of just a few days is sufficient to focus man's attention exclusively upon food. Even robust medical students, put into this experimental situation, cease to think and dream of the things they normally do, and instead think and dream only of food. Furthermore the starving state renders the individual restless. It is after a good meal that we sleep. It is when we are hungry that we become alert, preoccupied with thoughts of food and begin to forage. The restlessness of the severely starved anorectic is great both by day and night, and especially in the early hours of the morning. Starvation also turns her into a hoarder. A new streak of egocentricity and meanness emerges. "Shoplifting" may occur, rooted in this biological posture. Finally, if and when she surrenders to her impulse to eat, then it is her starvation that drives her to it.

It is to protect herself, within this catch 22 situation, that she develops complex patterns of secondary behaviour which, as previously described, characterize the established clinical state. She may take over control of cooking within the household, maintaining a tight rein on what is cooked and who eats what. Other members of the family often gain weight in their attempts to fit in with this sometimes seemingly desirable behaviour of the anorectic. However, she may also surround her own eating with elaborate rituals rooted in calorie counting and the consumption of her own sparse portions of food. She may insist on eating alone and in secret. If she surrenders to eating a greater amount than is consonant with maintaining her low body weight, then she may well need to be able to excuse herself immediately after the meal in order to vomit and/or to purge. Such absences immediately after the meal (the vomiting itself being effectively concealed) appear to escape the attention of many an anorectic's family, at least in terms of their actual significance. Such eating may also increasingly occur during the hours of the night. The desperation of her plight is such that she needs to manipulate all around her effectively and totally. Such stubbornness is often mistakenly identified by others as reflecting a streak of newfound autonomy and independence.

Excessive exercising may dominate the scene. The anorectic welcomes her biologically given restlessness and capitalizes upon it. She prefers to be active. She may undertake specific exercises or, as previously mentioned, walk or cycle long distances. Exercise, she knows, reduces body weight.

Even when severely debilitated at low body weight she may continue to exercise in this way. Such fitness at very low body weights is associated more with sustained carbohydrate avoidance coupled with ingestion of reasonable amounts of other foods rather than with the bingeing/vomiting/purging syndrome (which leads to much more widespread metabolic disturbances).

Many anorectic schoolgirls and students continue to strive in their schoolwork. The elements contributing to this may include (i) a fundamental need for academic achievement (as an aspect of the under-lying family psychopathology) which the anorexia nervosa is assisting through its stifling of the otherwise conflicting maturational process; (ii) the fact that concentration on school work often seems to be one of the few devices whereby preoccupation with food and eating can be held at bay for a while.

The family's experience of and view of their anorectic offspring is now focussed on her starving state, its implication for them and its challenge to their caring feelings. Any explicit or implicit adolescent or personal marital crisis of yesteryear is forgotten or may never have been recognized or acknowledged either by the anorectic or them. They are now confronted by the stark evidence of the anorexia nervosa. Their feelings may be of anger (they are powerless to alter the present obviously dangerous situation), or shame (it is fundamental to a mother to be able to feed and to be seen as able to feed her child), or despair. In some way or other the crisis in the individual is likely to be mirrored in them. Consciously they may seek only their daughter's recovery. They may remain mystified by her "problem". Such mystification bodes ill for their capacity ever to relate differently to their daughter.

In time many anorectics become separate from their parents for one reason or another. They may become estranged. The parents will die. The anorectic may remain socially isolated and emotionally stifled, or she may engage in a marriage. Such marriages are usually very restricted affairs. A man who marries an anorectic is marrying a strange person; someone who presumably meets his own needs for a barren and usually nonexistent sexual relationship, and who may be concerned primarily in feeding him up. He will be unaware of "the other side of her nature" having almost certainly engaged to win her either within the context of her developing anorexia nervosa (and hence with a causal contribution probably related to sexual and to role problems), or after she has developed it. Such relationships can occasionally have a mutually sustaining aspect, but more often than not, as he naturally matures (even slightly) over the years, the relationship becomes increasingly unsatisfactory to him. Conflict or rejection may then precipitate her into seeking help. On the other hand, if he does not change then any efforts on her part to struggle free from the condition may jeopardize their relationship and hence abort her search for help. Finally, so far as experiential aspects are concerned, sadness, hopelessness and, as previously mentioned, very occasionally something approaching ecstasy, can arise. When present, the depression and despair of anorexia nervosa is often related to a persistance of low self-esteem *despite* the anorectic posture. Alternatively, it may stem increasingly from the desperation born of awareness of the precariousness of low body weight control mechanisms available to the anorectic. Many anorectics feel constantly, like the alcoholic, that they are just one temptation away from disaster. If they once start eating they will never be able to stop. When suicide occurs it is often within this context. The individual is seeking relief from such endless terror and the exhaustion of the constant battle to maintain her position.

An Explanation of the Physical Features of Anorexia Nervosa

Detailed concern with the secondary physical complications of anorexia nervosa is not the purpose of this book. Secondary physical complications are those stemming from maintenance of low body weight by one or other dietetic device rather than the primary psychobiological mechanisms mobilized by the initial experiential needs of the individual.

These secondary physical complications stem from (i) dietary peculiarities, (ii) abuse of purgatives, diuretics and sometimes other drugs, (iii) the accompanying chronic starvation.

(i) Those relating to dietary peculiarities. So long as specific carbohydrate starvation is predominant then residual physical health is relatively well assured until very low body weights have been achieved, and so long as intake of other foods is not very excessive. However, excess consumption of protein can lead to poisoning of the body since the kidneys cannot handle the excess load. Some anorectics consume large quantities of carotene (a pigment found in carrots, green leafy vegetables, egg yolk, etc.) and turn orange in colour but without major detriment to their health. Absent intake of carbohydrate punctuated by carbohydrate binges can especially lead to striking disorders of fat metabolism that can be detected at the level of blood chemistry in this condition. Once bingeing and vomiting supervene as an established pattern then physical complications of a different order emerge. In contrast to the typical small stomach of the abstaining anorectic, the anorectic who begins to eat and drink very large quantities of food and water and then vomits may get severe dilatation of the stomach. If vomiting is excessive then dehydration, abdominal pain, fainting and other such complications supervene.

(ii) Drug abuse. Many anorectics consume large quantities of purgatives. These drugs, acting on the terminal bowel, often in the absence of any faecal mass (since food may have been vomited if eaten at all) produces a watery mucoid and sometimes blood-stained diarrhoea, which contains large amounts of body protein and essential substances such as potassium. Body stores of these substances begin to fall and serious symptoms arise. General weakness may be accompanied by specific cardiac and neurological defects. It is under these conditions that symptomatic epilepsy and collapse from a variety of causes usually stem.

Consumption of excess amounts of diuretics (drugs promoting output of urine) produces particularly severe dehydration (drying out of the body). This state increasingly terrifies the anorectic since now she only has to drink fluid in order to replace "permanent" weight. Moreover, it too becomes potentially life threatening, depending upon the particular diuretic used.

(iii) The effects of chronic starvation. The emaciated anorectic is, biologically speaking, a fraction of a person with qualitative biological defects. Reproductive capacity is eliminated. Food intake may be insufficient to sustain the remaining metabolic process and this, coupled with loss of insulating subcutaneous fat, leads to a fall in and a shut down of peripheral circulation, reflected in cold hands and feet. Cardiac output adaptively reduces and blood pressure and pulse rate drop to levels which are significantly below those necessary to sustain the biologically growing or mature individual, but which are "normal" to the individual concerned. The fine, downy hair which develops in many anorectics and characterizes other chronically starving populations, can perhaps be seen as having a body heat conservancy role.

The chronic starvation of anorexia nervosa, in the absence of bingeing and vomiting, leads as has already been said to a small wasted stomach and small bowel which, for instance, produces significantly less in the way of digestive juices and contains significantly fewer secretory glands than normal.

All of these features are reversible by full renourishment, even after many years.

Completely reversible also are the major hormonal abnormalities, especially those concerned with sexual and reproductive behaviour and which I believe are central to the nature of the disorder, both characterizing it and providing an essential biological mechanism within its development as a response to the primary psychopathology.

9
The Concept of it as Adaptive

The notion has been advanced that anorexia nervosa is a body weight-based phobic avoidance posture.

Without a doubt the commonest immediate entrée into the central mechanism of the condition is *carbohydrate avoidance*, stemming from a desire to reduce body size which has taken on new meaning following the latter's achievement of biological maturity. Body weight has by then become in the individual's mind a marker for the earlier initiation of puberty and is also a measure of current size and shape.

In my view dietary carbohydrate avoidance is a particularly powerful inhibitor of menstruation, in contrast to the effects of generalized protein calorie deprivation such as occurs in the Third World, and in other mechanisms of low body weight control within anorexia nervosa such as bingeing and vomiting. Such inhibition, often reflected almost immediately in a missed period and subsequently sustained amenorrhoea, is not always experienced as adaptive by the individual concerned, and may even induce anxiety; for instance if it is vaguely or suspiciously misconstrued as due to pregnancy by the anorectic or those around her. Many anorectics-to-be remain unconcerned. It is beyond this point that carbohydrate avoidance usually becomes very extreme in incipient anorexia nervosa. In the author's view the great majority of anorectics now find carbohydrate avoidance highly rewarding over this phase of their body weight loss, extending from say 100–88 lbs (45–40 kg). There are obviously exceptions to this weight range. My colleagues and I have found a very precise threshold within it for the majority of anorectics. However, anorexia nervosa can develop at substantially lower weights, especially in those who are very short, and in them the threshold in question is obviously lower. Somewhere precisely for them within this phase the central biological mechanisms deep in the brain governing sex hormone activity are "switched off". *Regression* is occurring.

The major and qualitative experiential changes which accompany and follow this are associated with a deep sense of relief which thereafter characterizes the maintenance of this avoidance posture. In contrast, thereafter, any approach back towards this threshold weight or movement into the critical and narrow range of body weight that reflects major rekindling of related hormonal processes and their experiential aspects, is associated with intense panic and then intensification of the avoidance mechanisms. These inevitably are directly reflected in dietetic behaviour wherein carbohydrate avoidance or else vomiting of ingested foods is reinforced.

In behaviouristic terms and perhaps limiting oneself to the concept of adult weight phobia as such, avoidance, or else vomiting of ingested food, can be said to be being *rewarded* or *reinforced* as a pattern of behaviour. In psychoanalytic terms such behaviour is *over-determined* by the multiplicity of its significances, through the mechanism of pubertal body weight threshold, in terms of growth, sexuality, separation, and the full spectrum of identity formation tasks for that individual, which are symbolized by the biological process. As the emerging anorectic rapidly *regresses* into her re-acquired, restricted and simpler existence, she experiences a sense of renewed *control* over her destiny and a renewed experience of safety. Adolescent chaos and actual or potential conflict have melted away, and so long as she can hold her new position she is secure. During times of special success in this it is, paradoxically, experienced as a sense of *greater autonomy* as well as security. This, in my view, has mistakenly led others to consider the disorder as primarily rooted in this experience, so that the *pivotal* significance of the pubertal process and the *avoidance* mechanism at work in relation to it is not recognised. For the anorectic herself such avoidance is rarely conceptualized as such, either during its enactment or thereafter. Indeed, such conceptualization would be inconsistent with her low level of thought organization, within which she thinks in mainly preverbal terms, perceiving only the biological reality and consequences of her stance. It is also consistent with her need to conceal this stance from the world. Meanwhile, her adolescent existential anxiety has been erased and replaced by a total fear-driven concern about maintaining her low weight, and hence a low level of effective ingestion of food. For this, control not only of herself but also of her environment is essential. The only freedom left to her is the apparent freedom to maintain her low body weight (Fig. 15).

Although the vast majority of anorectics achieve their adjustment in

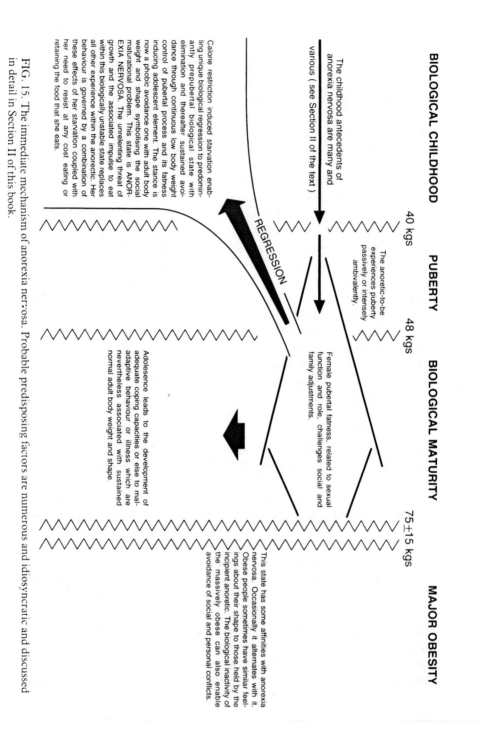

BIOLOGICAL CHILDHOOD — PUBERTY — BIOLOGICAL MATURITY — MAJOR OBESITY

The childhood antecedents of anorexia nervosa are many and various (see Section II of the text)

The anoretic-to-be experiences puberty passively or intensely ambivalently.

40 kgs

48 kgs

75±15 kgs

REGRESSION

Female pubertal fatness, related to sexual function and role, challenges social and family adjustments.

Calorie restriction induced starvation enabling unique biological regression to predominantly prepubertal biological state with elimination and thereafter sustained avoidance through continuous low body weight control of pubertal process and its fatness inducing adolescent element. The stance is now a phobic avoidance one with adult body weight and shape symbolising the social maturational problem. This state is ANOREXIA NERVOSA. The unrelenting threat of growth and the associated impulse to eat within this biologically unstable state replaces all other experience within the anorectic. Her behaviour is governed by a combination of these effects of her starvation coupled with her need to resist at any cost eating or retaining the food that she eats.

Adolesence leads to the development of adequate coping capacities or else to maladaptive behaviour or illness which are nevertheless associated with sustained normal adult body weight and shape.

This state has some affinities with anorexia nervosa. Occasionally it alternates with it. Obese people sometimes have similar feelings about their shape to those held by the incipient anoretic. The biological inactivity of the massively obese can also enable avoidance of social and personal conflicts.

FIG. 15. The immediate mechanism of anorexia ner·osa. Probable predisposing factors are numerous and idiosyncratic and discussed in detail in Section II of this book.

this way, there are a very few who more non-specifically drift downwards in body weight. These are far fewer in number than is popularly believed to be the case, since many typical anorectics succeed in denying for many years their active slimming intent. However there is a real, though very small, sub-group whose weight loss is initially related to true loss of appetite and reduced food intake arising in association with despair, panic, low sense of self-esteem, and not specifically focussed in the first instance on preoccupation with body shape and weight. However, as a low pre-pubertal body weight is reached then the secondary rewards of this are also experienced and serve to endorse the state. Such anorectics, with adult weight phobia arising relatively late in the day, often seem to be those whose existential crisis has been not so much a recent adolescent issue as a more long term one, characterizing also their childhood. It is as if the earlier weight/maturity threshold which had precipitated them out of the womb and into life in the outside world, and within which they had never found security even as a child, or a sense of being valued and of being of worth, had served to sensitize them to this next body-weight based insult of puberty, which is now requiring of them that they individuate even more. Bereft of childhood and now also of adolescent support resources of a kind they could utilize, their present condition reflects a more generalized retreat from growth and indeed from existence itself—a state of "giving up". In the past it may be that apparent failure to thrive and recover from debilitating diseases such as tuberculosis, often arising in adolescence, was partly at least related to the low body weight consequent on this condition, which held its secret rewards and necessary refuge for those individuals whose adolescent problems were otherwise overwhelming. Perhaps the increase in anorexia nervosa of the kind that we know today is partly related to the absence of such more natural protections as were previously afforded by chronic illnesses leading to major weight loss.

SECTION IV
Intervention and Self-help

10
Making the Diagnosis

Reference has already been made in Chapters 2 and 3 to the difficulties in reaching the diagnosis. Confirmation of the diagnosis usually requires a very difficult evaluation at several levels. On the other hand, clues to the existence of the condition within a person are often readily evident to anyone sensitive to the possibility. These days it can be suspected in anyone emaciated, especially of course young women with the typical cluster of behaviours. Sometimes the emaciation is not great but the person's struggle to curb food intake and preoccupation with it is still characteristic.

The diagnosis needs to be established at three levels. At the first and most superficial level are the evident physical and behavioural characteristics outlined in the first section of Chapter 2. At the second level, which in my view is the central and exclusive diagnostic level, the existence of the individual's need to maintain her low body weight and her terror of weight gain—her phobic avoidance stance in relation to normal adult body weight and, for her, its attendant fatness, needs to be established. Thus the essence of anorexia nervosa is not only the erstwhile presence of intense distress concerning adult body weight and shape but includes the essential element of phobic avoidance of this experience. This classical, and in this case biologically sustained, avoidance stance, otherwise equivalent in many ways to the social avoidance stance of the agoraphobic, is underpinned by a basic ambivalence to the feared "object". Thus, the positive pull of the anorectic towards this object is compounded of the normal thrust within the starved underweight organism to eat, and thus to survive, grow and restore biological maturity, coupled with any residual hope of social acceptance at this level. The negative pull is the overriding terror of re-exposure to this possibility.

In most ordinary social and clinical situations this complex state of mind can only be inferred since the individual denies its existence.

Occasionally it is more readily accessible to direct enquiry. Only if the individual is on the brink of spontaneous recovery will it be mentioned readily. A clinical analogy is the characteristic of the alcoholic, other drug addicts and sometimes the obese, to persistently deny and often effectively to minimize evidence of their true consumption.

The phobia is more likely to be revealed within a potentially thera-peutic first encounter which demands skills such as those possessed by clinically trained personnel who have become engaged with a potential "patient" with anorexia nervosa. Such an all-important encounter will contain within itself the seeds of possible effective therapy, and is likely also to lead to some preliminary adequate evaluation of the specific basis of the phobia (the meaning of the premorbid experience of biological maturation) for the individual concerned. At this level the formulation is on experiential, behavioural and social terms. It requires an evaluation of (i) the previous experience of "fatness" for the individual in terms of the body part and its particular meaning. (ii) The individual's potential coping resources as evidenced in childhood and also during that element of post-pubertal life that existed prior to the onset of the condition; it is a grave error at this stage to attempt to evaluate the patient's potential personality on the basis of her current behaviour and experience of this. This latter is predominantly driven by the posture of starvation which is common to all anorectics and indeed to all starved people. Experience is universally reduced to problems of ingestion which must never be construed as symbolically reflecting previous family relationships especially with the mother. The only surviving element of previous personality development still within the starved anorectic will be expressed in terms of the balance between her ritualized restraint of eating on the one hand and her "acting out" bingeing and vomiting on the other hand. (iii) The social setting, both in family and peer relation-ship terms. This latter will require appropriate clinical approaches to be made to the other people concerned. As previously stated, the structure of the family/peer psychopathology contains many elements that are not exclusive to the condition but which, in my view, *always* exist.

Details of the nature of this total approach to the problem of diagnosis and its possible and potential "treatment" implications are contained in the next chapter.

Other constitutional elements of both a social and biological kind in the individual and her family should be sought in the initial diagnostic encounter. As previously stated, though they characterize the condition they are neither exclusive to it or necessary for its development. They include a tendency amongst families to sustain middle class value systems, to contain other members with anorexia nervosa, or with difficulty over or excessive preoccupation with normal body weight regulation. The fathers of individuals with anorexia nervosa who binge and vomit are more often rigid and unbending. Parents are more likely than others to have themselves experienced significant degrees of depression in times past, and the mother in particular to have been characterized by social anxiety. Such "clinical" states reflect, in my view, related adjustments and reactions within such families which are important for the fuller understanding of their present problems.

Also as previously stated, within the individual with anorexia nervosa there is significantly often a history of plumpness, the existence of which or the degree of which may be concealed. The tendency for having been compliant or shy as a child is usually easily elicited. The occupation of the individual and her family members can be significant. Males chronically ill with the condition have a tendency to work as chefs or barmen or in some other nurturent capacity. Females have the same tendency but, as previously mentioned, are also often found to be training or employed as nurses, beauticians, nutritionists or involved in the health food business, or alternatively engaged in the world of fashion, theatre or the dance. Often such dedication is severely hampered or aborted because of chronic ill-health.

The Differential Diagnosis

The task of excluding other possible diagnoses can be most complicated. The undifferentiated and condensed thinking processes within anorexia nervosa coupled with the bizarre behaviour can readily lead some to consider the possibility of schizophrenia, a condition not in fact especially related to anorexia nervosa. The insistent statement of an anorectic that "my food is alive", or "I am being poisoned by my food" reflects undifferentiated cognitive processes and low order ideation which appear "psychotic" in quality and yet are often directly, bio-logically and experientially meaningful, and which sometimes yield to interpretation and to treatment of the anorexia nervosa. The existence of intense ritualistic behaviour, alcoholism, depression, all in fact secondary to the unerlying process, may instead become the focus of clinical concern. The generation of periodic massive oedema, of epilepsy and of other complex secondary metabolic/hormone abnormalities, and the evolution of secondary but profound gastro-intestinal disturbance such as frequent vomiting, abdominal pain, gastric dilatation, massive purgation and its effects, can all lead to misdiagnosis in the sense that the underlying condition goes unrecognized. Many years ago, working with a general physician/endocrinologist, I "found" about 30 such cases within one female ward which had about 2400 admissions over a three-year period.

Diagnosis within the male is usually more difficult, such that it may be assumed that the prevalence of the condition amongst males is greater than presently recognized, although almost certainly it remains much more rare amongst them than amongst females. Even those who may more readily and accurately diagnose its presence in a female often do not expect to encounter it in the male. Male clothing more effectively masks the true degree of emaciation. Absence of menstruation is irrelevant. Amongst those males with anorexia nervosa who reach the clinic there is a greater proportion who habitually overeat and vomit than there is amongst the female population of "anorectics". Alcoholism is more common within the condition and the social class background is less often middle class. A more evident premorbid phase of impulsive and sometimes delinquent behaviour has often existed.

11
Attempting to Create an Opportunity for Development and Change—the Kindling Process

Early on in this book I have suggested that there might be real advantages as well as theoretical justifications in imposing the conventional "illness" model upon anorexia nervosa. These must be in the realm of treatment—the capacity to intervene in a way that alters the course of the "illness" for the better. Such a notion invites and indeed demands further questions, e.g. for the better of whom—"the patient", the "patient's" family, the doctor? Whose security, comfort and judgements about lifestyle are at stake?

There is no doubt that medical intervention in anorexia nervosa can sometimes be effective in the short term—in the sense of preserving life when the condition is severe and otherwise terminal. The "patient" may still be strenuously resistant to such intervention but the matter is usually taken out of her hands by the social impact of the crisis. The patient is physically weak, often weighing 30 kg or less, hardly able to stand, feebly protesting, the family doctor comes urgently upon the scene, an ambulance is mobilized, first aid medical care is initiated, intravenous drips are set up. Under these conditions, providing a correct chemical approach is made to the metabolic abnormalities now present, for example bearing in mind the urgent need of the body for glucose and yet the often present profound potassium depletion which may be further deranged by just such intervention—then life may be saved. Such intervention usually can do little but stave off further crises.

To attempt to alter the course of the disorder in a more substantial way a more profound intervention is necessary. Many ask "Can this ever be completely successful?" The answer is Yes—sometimes. Firstly, people with anorexia nervosa can be helped through an otherwise terminal state of the condition as described above, and then eventually recover. In the simplest instance, refeeding within a caring nursing environment can very occasionally be sufficient. In my view this is only likely to happen if the immediately prior severe deterioration has occurred within the context of threatened spontaneous recovery, which the individual had sensed and been unable to face without a temporary shift of circumstances and role, such as admission to hospital provides. This same process often operates within the lives of those who so frequently present to hospital these days having taken overdoses of psychotropic drugs.

Other "mechanistic" interventions are also sometimes initiated, the impact of which needs to be evaluated taking into account also the impact of the related social conditions and their meaning for the patient and others, e.g. hospitalization, nursing care. These include the administration of drugs, hormones and electroconvulsive therapy.

Anorectics, of course, sometimes treat themselves with "drugs" or "hormones"—the intention being to sustain them in their battle to maintain their present condition. They may occasionally be using alcohol or sedatives. They may be dependent upon amphetamine-like compounds. They may be taking purgatives or diuretics. They may be taking thyroid-like hormones. They experience such drugs as helping them maintain their present situation and will be very resistant to abandoning their consumption.

Physicians if they are aware of such consumption often attempt to stop it. They may prescribe other drugs which in fact are rarely consumed if intended for introduction by mouth. They include drugs that may facilitate appetite, e.g. certain tricyclic compounds. Sometimes small doses of insulin are given by injection to increase appetite. I believe such drugs and hormones to be dangerous to the anorectic. They may lead to temporary weight gain through increased food intake, especially by those who have been resisting eating rather than overeating and vomiting, but the risk is run of converting such individuals into new low weight control systems of overeating and vomiting with all its more sinister long-term implications. Body-building steroids are sometimes given and are of no value. The intermittent administration of oestrogens may produce a semblance of gynaecological normality in those not severely underweight by provoking withdrawal menstrual bleeds but again, I believe these to be of no real value. Recently it has been suggested that a particular peptide found to profoundly influence appetite in the rat may pave the way to effective pharmacological intervention in anorexia nervosa. I doubt it. As I have reiterated previously, the anorectic does not eat, although she is often hungry, because she is terrified of gaining weight and of altogether losing control over food intake, thereby becoming grossly fat. A logical pharmacological approach to this—especially for those who overeat and vomit and who are most often acutely aware of such imminent disaster for themselves—might be to give them drugs that curb appetite, thereby making it safer for them to eat and retain a little more food. However there is no known drug intervention that can radically alter the course of the condition for the vast majority of anorectics.

We will go on to examine the possibilities of other social and behavioural manipulations and interventions and their experiential implications for the anorectic. It is my belief that a capacity to allow personal growth— a strengthening of the patient's and/or family's experiential resources, is crucial to their effectiveness. As with medical pharmacological intervention, such effects need to be evaluated against the background of the natural evolution of the condition, including spontaneous recovery as a possible outcome. It must be remembered that many anorectics only allow exposure of themselves to treatment when they are anyway on the brink of such recovery and can afford to have it facilitated. The evaluation of such "treatments" is therefore very difficult and has never been systematically undertaken. Presentation of the condition to doctors, the consequent need for presumed optimal treatment rather than calculated random allocation to a variety of types of treatment, and the problems of measuring meaningful change all militate against such study. After all it take decades to evaluate more specific procedures in medicine e.g. the effect of aspirin or steroids in arthritis, the effect of radical surgery on cancer of the breast.

So far as anorexia nervosa is concerned, I recommend stringent criteria for those seeking to proclaim successful intervention in the condition. At one level, of course, is the capacity to enhance survival although the illness still persists. This has been touched on earlier in the chapter in respect of intervention in the otherwise terminal state. Other than within this context, interventions within the illness, even if consciously aimed at enhancing well-being, should be approached with caution. As with drug treatments, refeeding through nursing care or behavioural manipulation (e.g. confining the half-resistant patient to bed and rewarding weight gain with greater freedom) apart from its humanly degrading aspects, may lead eventually to a deterioration of the condition in relation to that which would otherwise have naturally occurred. By adopting a stark mechanistic and manipulative approach one is often merely reconfirming for the anorectic her earlier experiences of life.

Anorectics, if invited to nominate an ideal weight for themselves, will often admit a willingness to be somewhere around 6 to 6½ stones (38–41 kg). Under such circumstances the would-be therapist is wise to recognize that such a weight, or even some other lower weight in say those who are very short, is an immediately sub-pubertal one and the maximum naturally safe one for the anorectic individual. As described earlier, the lower weight that now characterizes her has been arrived at as an added insurance against exceeding the former weight. Any intervention that unthinkingly temporarily promotes the anorectic's weight towards it, at the same time threatens food intake control mechanisms and does not help her meaningfully through the weight into the reaches of a mature biological weight, may in the longer term promote instead a greater retreat from it as soon as the individual is again in charge of her own food intake and weight control mechanisms.

It is to this question—as to how outside "help" can be given to enable the anorectic to break out of the condition—that this chapter will now be addressed.

Such help may be primary and intentional, or secondary to symptomatic treatments and often unintentional. Thus, to take the latter category first, the intervention of someone or some team of caring people outside the patient's immediate environment may automatically create important new social situations and experiences for the anorectic which may be therapeutic to some extent. Such care and interest combined with firmness over limited goals concerning weight gain is often attempted and can occasionally be helpful.

The anorectic, of course, partially "trapped" in such a situation, will usually initially have developed a very clear view of the amount of weight she must gain as the price for diminished concern by others, which will once more allow her her freedom. Often she knows a few kilograms will suffice.

Central to the task of helping the anorectic is that of also involving or helping the parents or others importantly concerned with them. Parents will often feel helpless and angry. They will have spent endless fruitless hours together or singly trying to encourage, bully, cajole their daughter to eat. They may have become as expert in their own way as she is— furtively stocking the refrigerator—aware of her many idiosyncracies—all to no avail. They may be more united or divided than before, usually the former, but nevertheless helpless in the face of the problem. The mother in particular feels the shame of not being able to feed her child adequately. She may not be privy to the latter's concern about her weight. So far as the mother is concerned, the emaciated daughter may be solely an explicit statement to others that she, the mother, is in some way grossly inadequate.

Parents need to be helped to a greater understanding of the problem, they need to grasp their own importance in the matter and to become involved. They need to construe their new roles reflecting their responsibilities rather than their blame. They need compassionate help, perhaps allowing them to see that we all have our Achilles' heel and that this just happens to be theirs as individuals and as a family.

One cannot be involved in the business of anorexia nervosa for long without being starkly confronted by the problem of free will versus determinism. Is the anorectic free to chose an alternative way of life or is she simply a product of biological forces and previous social experiences. We tend to see other people's attitudes and behaviour as shaped by life and predetermined, our own as operating in relation to our "will". Can the anorectic chose to confront her illness? Why do we need her to do so? In everyday clinical practice these questions can hopefully be in one's mind. Hopefully that is because they are likely to contain the seeds of the necessary "kindling process" for the anorectic.

The procedure in our clinical service is rooted in the notion that the anorectic or some part of her must wish for change and escape from the illness for this to be a therapeutic possibility. The therapeutic task is (i) to enlarge her experience of herself as she is, and usually for her family to attempt the same; (ii) to provide her, and often them, with new experiences facilitating personal growth—a growing capacity to cope with herself in life, biologically mature and without recourse to anorexia nervosa.

For this to happen in a way that transcends natural development it will usually be important for those around her to cope with similar changes in themselves. The alternative is for such changes to be sought totally outside the family environment and hence totally within the therapeutic environment—an especially daunting task for the individual with the condition and for those trying to help her. Sometimes such a task is necessary and can be undertaken on the basis about to be described. The dangers of working only with the anorectic are most clearly revealed within the classical psychoanalytic approach. This, in my view, suffers from a failure to recognize the biologically regressive basis of anorexia nervosa. The anorectic enters the psychoanalytic treatment alliance within her regressed and starved state. The alliance unwittingly fosters the regression, concentrating on the presumed direct symbolic significance of eating in terms of the mother/child relationship, instead of

identifying the underlying and now avoided post-pubertal psychopathology of body shape. Parents are often excluded from meaningful
involvement in therapy and the anorectic sustains her regression and her
illness in the face of mistaken transference interpretations. The anorectic
and sometimes those around her must be prepared for the experience of
painful feelings. Without anorexia nervosa they may be different,
perhaps wiser but probably also sadder in the first instance at least.

The initial encounter, so far as I am concerned, is usually in the out-
patient department of the psychiatric unit. However, it could equally
well be within the general practitioner's consulting room, the physician's
out-patient department, or within the contact characteristically provided
by some other helping agency. If a non-medical helping agency was
involved then obviously there would need to be links with a medical
service because of the problems of differential diagnosis and also those of
the medical aspects of management of the anorexia nervosa, should this
latter diagnosis be confirmed.

In certain ways anorectics and their families find it less difficult than
some to contemplate psychiatric evaluation. The family is often
desperate and they may themselves be convinced that the illness is
psychologically based, even if in fact they have misjudged the true nature
of its experiential basis. However, this encounter with a psychiatrist can
still often be difficult for them for the usual reasons. Thus they may see it
as an acknowledgement of defeat and of weakness, they may also fear the
attention about to be directed at their personal lives. For the anorectic
herself there is in addition the overriding fear that she may be expected
or in some way compelled merely to gain weight.

It is probably best to meet the parents or other involved people first.
This allows an initial perspective on the condition by those involved but
also outside it, and it can also make plain from the outset the *expectation*
that the family too must now be involved in any treatment that
transpires. If two parents are together in the consultation they may
between them be able to provide quite an accurate history of the
condition, monitoring each other's memories and views. They may be
more anxious to talk about the "illness" and about the chances of
something helpful being *done to the patient* than about themselves. Many
are able to talk about themselves, each other and their relationship if
appropriately helped to do so, although the interviewer will be confronted
by their potential for denial. Thus although middle age is a time when
some of us are more able to reconsider ourselves, our attitudes and our
lifestyles, or else may begin to surrender to personal destinies which have

been resisted since adolescence, the anorectic's family is often characterized, at least within the context of the patient's illness, as unbending. Meanwhile, constant recourse by them to self-blame should be treated with respect and, at this stage, reassurance along the lines that they are correct in bel eving that they are importantly involved, after all are they not the parents, transmitting heredity and conferring their early hopes, aspirations and other needs upon their children's development.

It will be important to begin to learn about their natures, their strengths and the defects they see in themselves, in each other and in their relationship, the latter's ups and downs. They may need particular help not to resort habitually to denying them. What are the values by which they live, how do they differ in this respect from each other, in what ways do their children take after the one or other of them? Which aspects of their children do they prize? What are their aspirations for them individually? How did they observe their children coping with puberty? How did they help their children in this? As parents discuss and reflect on such issues they can become more aware of their own roles in the family and in the development of the disorder. The nature of their relationship emerges, the ways in which they avoid or smother conflict, the alliances they make with their parents, with each other and with their children. In particular parents may be helped to see that their attitudes and any undue rigidity are importantly a product of their own early lives and, through nonjudgemental inspection of this, to come to view themselves more realistically. All is no longer idealized or rejected. Any such initial slight changes of perspective contain the seedbeds of change in attitude to their adolescent children.

This initial meeting often allows the erection of some provisional hypotheses concerning the maturation problems that had confronted their now anorectic and regressed child. The meeting will have involved myself and an experienced social worker colleague. Often the latter will continue the meeting with the parents whilst I go on to the first meeting with the potential patient. Of course sometimes there will have been no prior meeting with other members of the family. They may not have been available or the anorectic may have prevented them attending despite the clinic's insistence on it.

Very occasionally an anorectic will herself be asking for real help— often as she approaches the age of 30 or thereabouts and becomes aware of the need to struggle free of the condition if at all possible. More often anorectics themselves desperately seeking help from doctors are actually hoping that the latter may be able to bring some temporary external controls to bear on their appetite, which has got out of their own control such that they are overeating and gaining weight. Their hope, that some temporary refuge will be provided until such times as they have lost the recently gained weight and re-established self-control in respect of low food intake, will be effectively concealed from the doctor or other person involved who may feel gratified that the anorectic seems to want to get better. However, such an alliance with medical and nursing care never survives beyond the point at which the anorectic has achieved her short term goals. Certainly any apparent and immediate successful attempt to promote even a little weight gain in such a patient will precipitately reveal the fear of it, even if this has been strenuously and convincingly denied previously.

Most often, however, one's first meeting with the anorectic in the out-patient department is initially characterized by her resistance to being there. The change from this attitude to her being prepared to contemplate real change in herself is a very big one.

Meanwhile her assessment of me, or any would-be patient's assessment of any new doctor, will be coloured by many misconceptions, but she will be very concerned to decide as soon as possible whether 'r not my exclusive concern is to try and make her put on weight. At this very early stage it is sometimes very helpful to point out to the anorectic that she is in danger of considering the doctor as someone similar to and with similar intentions to those of her parents. This early attempt to differentiate oneself from the parents (called in the jargon a kind of "early interpretation of the transference") is all important since the anorectic's regressed personality structure, generally poor capacity to discriminate, leading to her artificially splitting people into "good" and "bad", and all her recent experience will lead her to expect that the doctor will not only collude with others but is actually like others in merely wishing for her to gain weight and thus seem well once more. Such an interpretation will of course not exert any magical effect in itself, but will merely provide a basis for more realistic communication with the anorectic *provided it is essentially true and thereby seen to be so by the anorectic herself.* The anorectic will soon test its validity and the therapist will inevitably be forced to re-examine his own views.

Since the anorectic, at least, may still be habitually denying many aspects of her condition it can, if the diagnosis is evidently not in doubt, be helpful to begin by describing anorexia nervosa, revealing some understanding of its adaptive purposes and the deceits to which this leads. Anorectics particularly welcome understanding being shown of their sometimes ever-present fear of loss of control of eating.

Some anorectics do see their condition as reflecting problems in growing up. In this first encounter it will be just as important to explore the family structure and the personalities and histories of those in it with her as it was with the parents. The bonds and alignments within the family, the impact of the patient's puberty upon it, the extent to which prior to her "illness" she was aware that within herself were elements of both her mother's and her father's natures, the incompatibility of these within the family, and the impact of the departure from the family of other siblings are amongst issues that merit particular attention.

The previous chapter was concerned with the various levels of diagnosis and differential diagnosis. The physical and behavioural aspects are usually relatively apparent or elicitable. The importance of establishing the existence of the *weight phobia*, apart from its diagnostic relevance, is that it provides an opportunity for the doctor or other person *to begin to talk the anorectic's language.* The weight phobia is not infrequently denied at this stage although it will sometimes be admitted, almost with relief, even by anorectics who have effectively concealed it for many years.

The history of the evolution of the phobia, its onset, its fluctuations and its final intensification will provide clues concerning cardinal other experiences in the development of the condition.

At the end of this first encounter with the patient and their family comes the question of treatment.

I usually present the possibilities in the following way: (i) The task, literally speaking, is to grow up—both biologically and psychologically. (ii) This may happen naturally and is more or less likely. An account of the illness with its possible outcome with particular reference to the patient's "case" should be provided here to all concerned (factors associated with good and bad outcome will be discussed in Chapter 14). (iii) If this evolution is to be modified then psychological change in the first instance can only come about with weight gain to normal adult levels. However, thereafter, further psychological change will need to occur and this is best achieved gradually. Rapid psychological change at this stage, once normal weight has been achieved, is likely to reflect primitive reactions and conversions and is often precarious.

Anorectics are terrified at such proposals. Their possible *facilitation* by us (not *implementation*, i.e. the anorectic needs to do it and we to help) is described in the following way. Firstly it is explained to all concerned that weight gain of the kind described above is a fundamental necessity. It is expected to and in most instances does promote those changes that have previously been experienced and recognized as puberty or at least its beginnings. We recognize that these changes are of a qualitative kind affecting both them and those around them. At the moment, being biologically incomplete, examination of the psychological issues surrounding their adult maturational problems is not possible since they and their family cannot experience any part of them through the anorectic and the present avoidance stance. We can help them to gain the necessary weight (we invite them at this stage to visit the unit and see other anorectics involved in the process) and *thereby also* help them begin to explore the psychological factors in a way that may enable them and others to deal with problems differently from before. The anorectic's freedom currently exists only in terms of manipulating weight, and in this sense too she is a prisoner since she is only precariously free to maintain her low body weight. Therapy will be concerned with creating freedoms of a personal and social kind (e.g. freedom to experience, recognize and share feelings and ideas, to explore relationships and to take risks as an adolescent) for the first time, concurrently with allowing physical growth to pursue its natural course.

A programme for gaining weight will be effected by them coming into hospital, going to bed, and being prescribed a 3000 calorie diet with normal amounts of carbohydrate and with a target weight equivalent to that of the matched population mean weight. This is the average weight within the population of people similar to themselves in terms of sex and height, but in fact of an age equivalent to that at which they had first fallen ill. Thus an anorectic aged 21 and ill since the age of 15 can see that she is being invited to pick up normal biological life again at the chronological point at which she withdrew from it. Thus she can perhaps grasp that she is being expected, in an emotional sense, once weight has been restored, to cope with being a 15-year-old and not a 21-year-old. The true complexity of the psychological task confronting her is thus made more concrete both for her and her family. Of course the older she now is chronologically the greater this task in general. However in my view it is the most that can be expected of her. Such weights, by age, are tabulated in Appendix Ia. They differ from so-called ideal body weights (an actuarial concept) by being age-related, increasing with it from puberty onwards.

Anorectics understand, and often acknowledge why they should be confined to bed. It allows the necessary element of control if weight gain is to occur without too much difficulty. They will again be terrified of surrendering such control to people they do not trust, and they will not do it unless they have at least some hope of more widespread help. They will be reassured if they learn that under no circumstances will anyone else, e.g. parents, be allowed to bring food in; nor will any extra food be allowed them from within the unit. The task is to gain the target weight, and then through a process of increasingly being up and about, and progressive re-allocation of responsibility back to them for control of their food intake, to hold it. This task in itself, even as a physiological exercise, is going to prove a daunting one for them and it is appropriate to acknowledge this at this stage.

Within such a treatment programme, concerned simply with this limited issue of body weight, it will usually require 8 to 12 weeks to achieve the target weight with the individual gaining approximately 1½ kg a week (Fig. 16). Following this preliminary presentation of the necessary treatment contract regarding weight gain the anorectic will almost certainly have developed major reservations about involving herself. It will now be important to talk about the other and equally fundamental element of treatment. She should be helped to see that the apparently repressive measures concerning weight gain are to be coupled with psychotherapy with both herself and those around her. She can

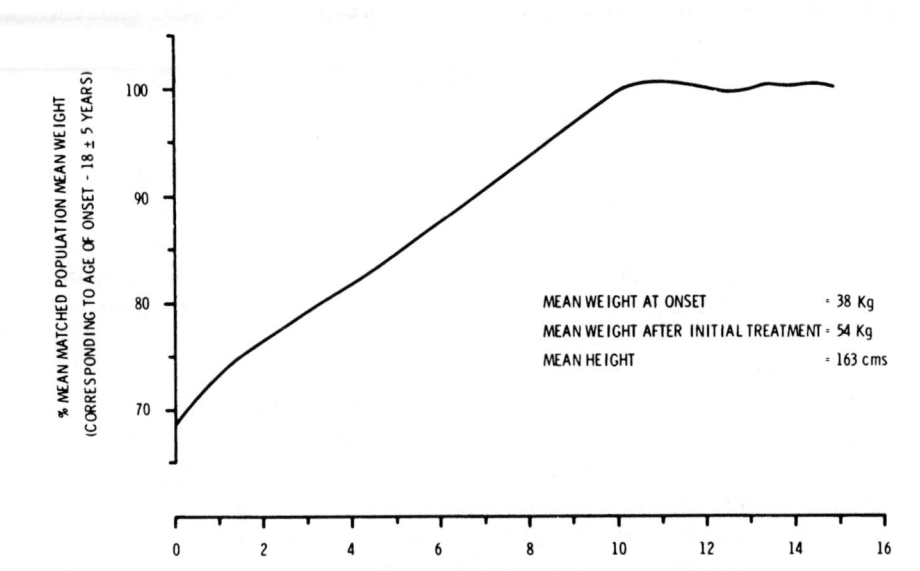

FIG. 16. The immediate effect of in-patient treatment on body weight in just over 300 patients severely ill with anorexia nervosa, who underwent this phase of care 1960–1978 (excluding 19 patients who discharged themselves during the process).

hope that others around her will also be expected to change in a psychological sense, and that indeed one of the purposes of the strict control exercised within that aspect of the treatment programme concerned with promoting weight is so as to bring this whole aspect of the disorder under such control as hopefully to allow greater freedom of thought in other directions.

It is a profound error to construe an anorectic's going to bed and eating in the way described above as regressive. It may potentially contain regressive elements of its own if not guarded against, but in the main it is a process the opposite of regression. Nothing is more regressed than the "free-ranging" anorectic. An anorectic who has *elected* to and is gaining weight is progressively confronting herself and others with the weight gain necessary for maturation to occur (Fig. 17). Only if she continues to feel that this is being *done to her* does it contain the elements of a passive experience, mirroring her past dependence and helplessness and perhaps also mirroring the experience of her first natural puberty.

Such a rigid programme as this concerned with the physical weight aspect of the problems is surely not the only approach to achieving the weight gain necessary for effective psychotherapy. However it is one which works, which allows numbers of anorectics to use our in-patient facilities at the same time because of its simplicity and apparent fairness, and always providing it is properly recognized that it is the anorectic who has made the decisions and who can therefore begin to take on the responsibility for her own body given this initial assistance.

The anorectic and the family at this stage may benefit from a further discussion of the essential nature of the psychotherapy proposed, and indeed they may already have experienced some of its elements through the processes of the present consultation and what is by now a meeting with all of them together. The nature of these processes will be described below, but at this stage it is often appropriate to put the important proposition to the anorectic and her family that she and they should go off at the end of the consultation and reflect on the treatment programme offered. They are invited to write in within a week or ten days indicating their decision as to whether or not they wish to engage in it. Such a decision should be as much a joint decision as possible although often in effect one or more members of the family may exercise pressure on the others either to accept or reject it. This personal commitment to a clearly defined treatment programme in the first instance is then a crucial element without which there is little prospect of real and long lasting change. The alternative is still that the anorectic and her family may pay lip service to such a contract and may even allow restoration of weight to normal levels, but in the anorectic's mind will be the ever-present notion that the price she is having to pay for disengagement from the situation in which she is now involved is gaining weight. She will come into hospital, gain the weight, and always retain the dominating thought that she will lose it, regressing quickly again as soon as she is discharged. This is not to say, of course, that such an attitude cannot still become modified at a later date if it is recognized. The anorectic and her family at this stage

FIG. 17. (a–e). These complicated and technical charts show the changes that occur in hormonal status as substantial body weight is gained towards normal mature adult levels.

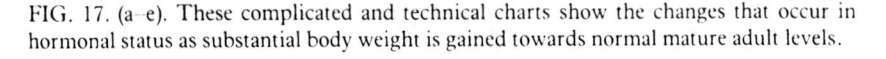

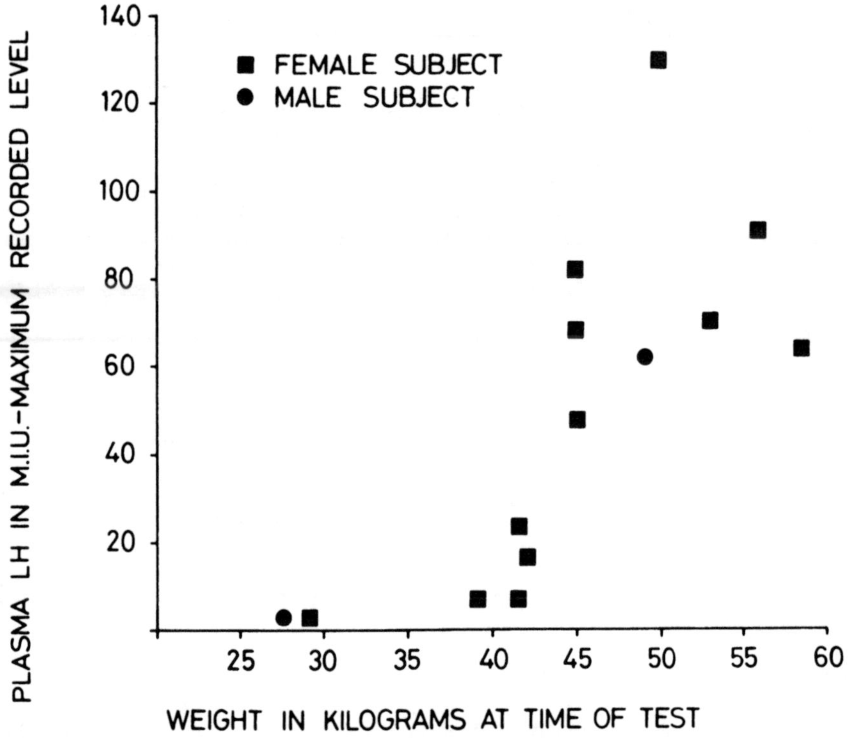

(a) shows the maximum luteinizing hormone (LH) response as measured by plasma level, to stimulation of the brain by a substance mirroring a natural hypothalamic agent. It can be seen that the pituitary gland was unresponsive to this stimulation so far as LH production was concerned when individuals weighed less than about 43 kg. This threshold, which must inevitably vary somewhat between individuals, probably mirrors early features of natural puberty long before menstruation sets in. Thus, whereas on average this threshold is of the order of 41–44 kg, the average weight at which menstruation returns in an anorectic population is several kg more.

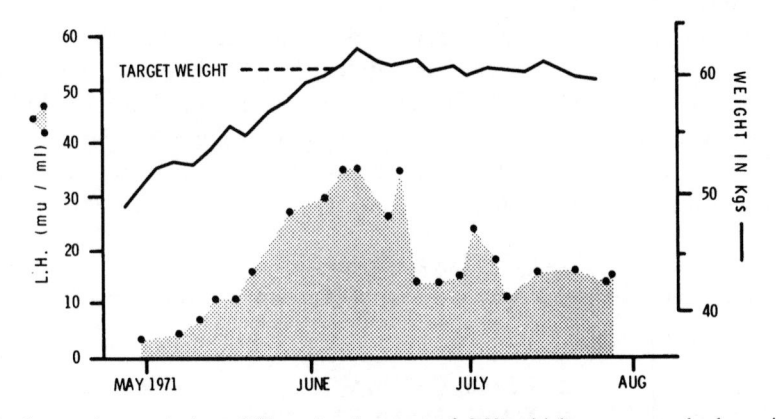

MISS A. 17yrs (Ht: 178cm)

(b) shows that typical undifferentiated surge of LH which occurs as body weight approaches the 46–50 kg mark. This surge is more typical of early puberty than of the later, well-organized spike of high LH which appears in the blood for about 48 hours in mid-menstrual cycle, heralding ovulation. As the anorectic gains weight and passes through this biological experience she will sometimes redevelop acne and begin to blush again like any young teenager in the grip of newly found sexual self-awareness. Such promptings may of course be denied both to the self and especially to others.

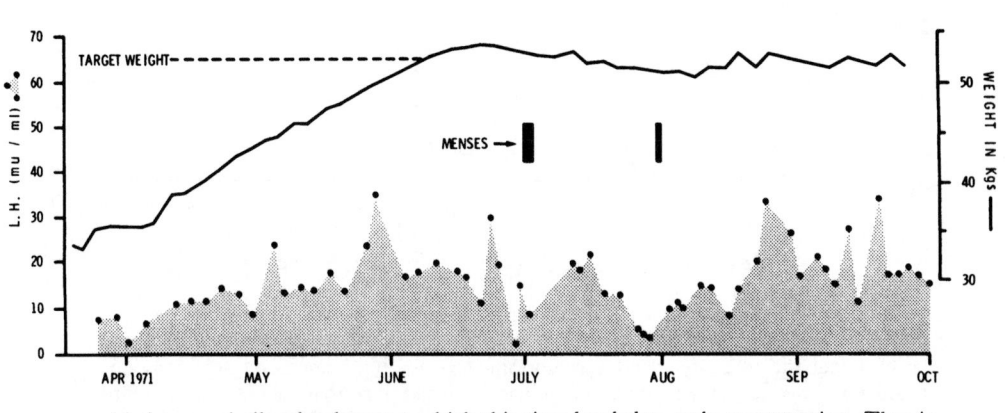

MISS B. 20yrs (Ht: 163 cm)

(c) shows a similar development which this time has led to early menstruation. Thus in this case it can be seen that the ovaries themselves had begun to function cyclically, leading to periodic surges of oestrogen in the plasma.

MRS C. 44yrs (Ht: 152cm)

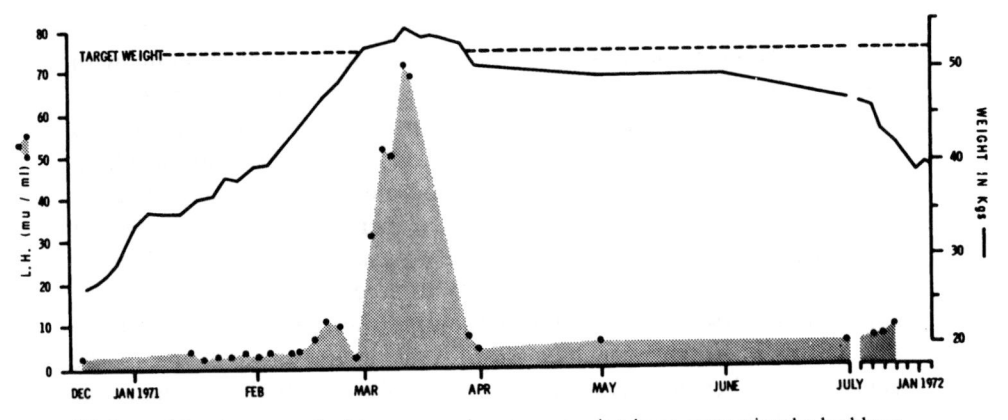

(d) shows this same surge, in this case a major one occurring in an anorectic who had been severely emaciated for over 25 years. It demonstrates that after all this time normal biological function is still possible. Despite this person's strenuous efforts and those of her would-be helpers, it can be seen that she was unable to sustain a normal weight.

MISS D. 15yrs (Ht: 158cm)

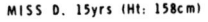

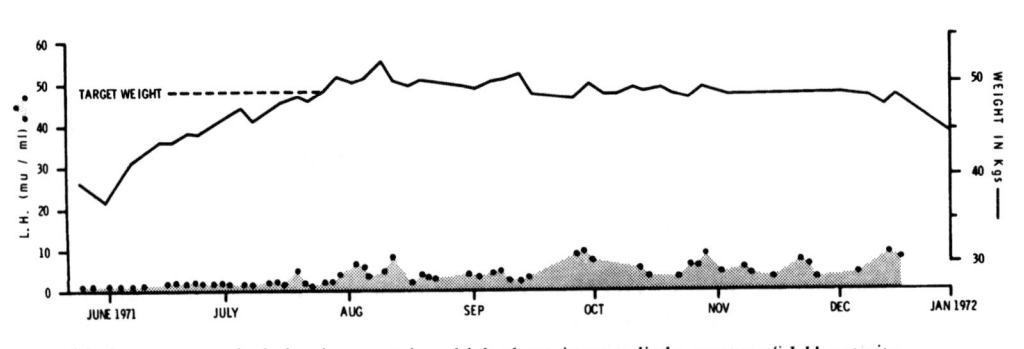

(e) shows an atypical development in which there is very little return of LH activity during the period under scrutiny despite the patient maintaining her target weight. She had been obese before she developed anorexia nervosa and had never had menstrual periods at a weight as low as her present target weight. It was some years before she began to menstruate at her newfound weight. Meanwhile she was presumably subject to the thrust of incomplete growth reflected in a continuing large appetite and a somewhat chaotic food intake.

Social Worker Involvement

One aspect of the social worker's involvement may have to do with her ability to organize such things as continuing education for the patient whilst she is in hospital, and her ability to organize accommodation for the patient on leaving hospital should this not otherwise be available or appropriate. The social worker may, along with others such as the nurse, the occupational therapist, the clinical psychologists or the doctor, be the appropriate person to be involved in an aspect of the formal psychotherapy which will be discussed shortly.

Schooling

Especially if the anorectic is of school age then the possibility of specific educational activities during the in-patient period needs to be considered. Specially qualified teachers are sometimes available but should only become involved as part of the treatment team.

Some anorectics will have faltered in their schooling a long while before admission. Others will have been working desperately and defensively hard right up until the day of admission. Some will have examinations arranged for the near future which they and/or their families believe to be of paramount importance.

Any schooling, whilst an in-patient, needs to be planned with full awareness that the hospital stay is going to involve the patient in great turmoil. The specific direction of previous academic strivings may be part and parcel of aspirations that were inappropriate and which are now being carefully examined within other aspects of therapy. Equally it will be premature to opt for alternative courses of study. More constructive than the intensive academic teaching of certain subjects during this period will be an introduction to topics of a more general educational, social and vocational kind.

The teacher may be able to take advantage of concurrent gains in psychotherapy which are enabling the patient to begin to be more openly reflective. Then the teacher will have an important role in contributing to the patient's attempts to exercise more mature and autonomous judgements. Teachers should be aware that during the period of weight gain up to normal levels the patient is undergoing qualitative changes of a physical kind. The usual experience for teachers of observing the impact of puberty on academic achievement spread over four years or more may be condensed instead into three months.

FIG. 18 a–g. These 7 paintings, each by a different anorectic, were produced during in-patient treatment as part of art therapy and were used within the on-going psychotherapy.

(a) The patient newly admitted and unable to show much emotion in the presence of other people, was invited to paint her feelings. She painted red and yellow flames smothered but barely so by a black crust.

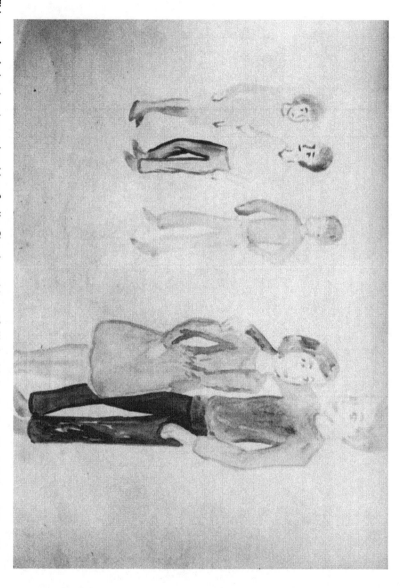

(b) This newly admitted patient painted her family. She showed herself allied with her husband and distanced from her parents. As she regained weight she began to paint herself moving towards her parents and away from her husband — a process that mirrored her changing needs at this time.

(c) Asked to paint the future this patient could only see it in terms of an uphill struggle over a series of cloud covered peaks. On reaching the summit (concretely identifiable as her target weight) she would relapse.

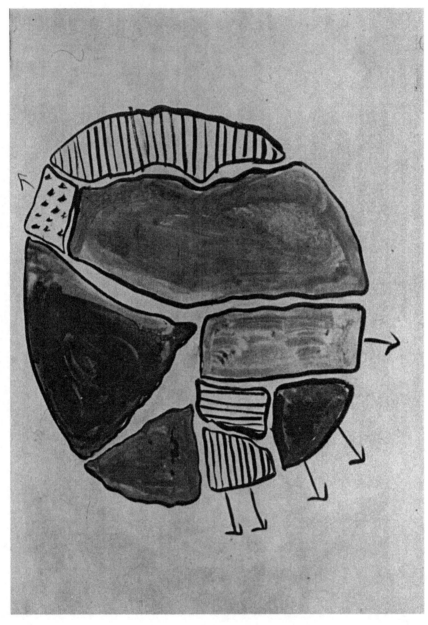

(d) Half-way towards target weight this patient painted herself as this fragmenting object.

(e) At target weight and asked to paint her feelings, this patient saw herself as about to be engulfed. In the event she continued to do well showing considerable resource in coping with the challenges in her life.

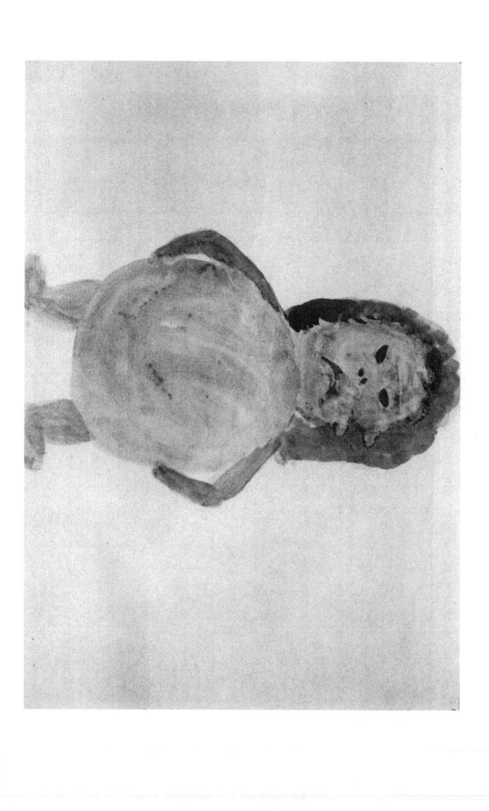

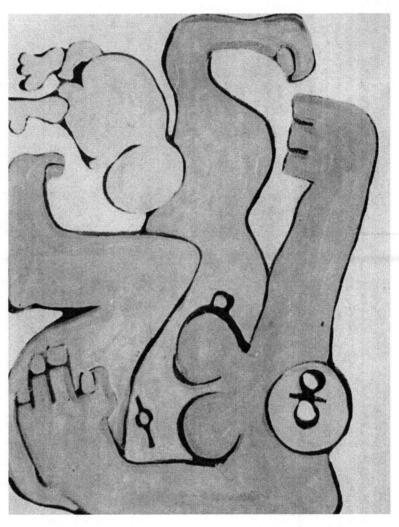

(f), (g) Patients painting themselves at target weight portray themselves as inflicted with obesity and sexuality and as being bad, ugly and resentful.

FIG. 19 a–h. This sequence of paintings was produced by one patient as she progressed through in-patient treatment during which time she was involved in individual psychotherapy and her weight rose from about 35 to 50 kg which was her target weight.

(a) Asked to paint her family she portrayed her two brothers playing ball. Watching them subservient but in the same arena and allowed to pick up the ball when it dropped, is her sister who until recently also had anorexia nervosa. Behind the tree, bottom right, is the childlike figure of the 24-year old patient, ten years an anorectic, separated off from her siblings. Above her is the formidable figure of her mother, separated from the rest of the family and especially from the isolated figure of the father on the left-hand side of the picture. Although the mother dominates the patient and, through the anorexia nervosa, retains the patient's allegiance and hence continues not to reject her, there is also a barrier between them. The patient saw this as due to their inability to share feelings and to the potential ambivalence within their relationship which would be acutely activated once the patient had gained weight and in other ways moved away from her anorectic stance.

(b) Asked to paint herself she sketches in a buffet supper table towards which everyone else, brightly coloured, is rushing. They can all participate in the pleasures of life. A band plays in the upper left-hand corner and the patient, a small black figure, dances by herself, exercising extreme self-control.

(c) Invited to paint friendship she had great difficulty because she said she had never experienced it. She saw friendship to be accepting her as she really was and to involve the sharing of feelings. She expressed surprise that others saw the couple as looking young, innocent and asexual. She was insistent that friendship and sex are mutually exclusive.

(d) As she gained weight she was asked to paint her feelings. She painted herself sitting and eating angrily at a table. People rushed towards her. Gaining weight made this inevitable and she felt that the others were commenting on her eating and her shape. Her anger would destroy something very close to her and this would lead to great sadness.

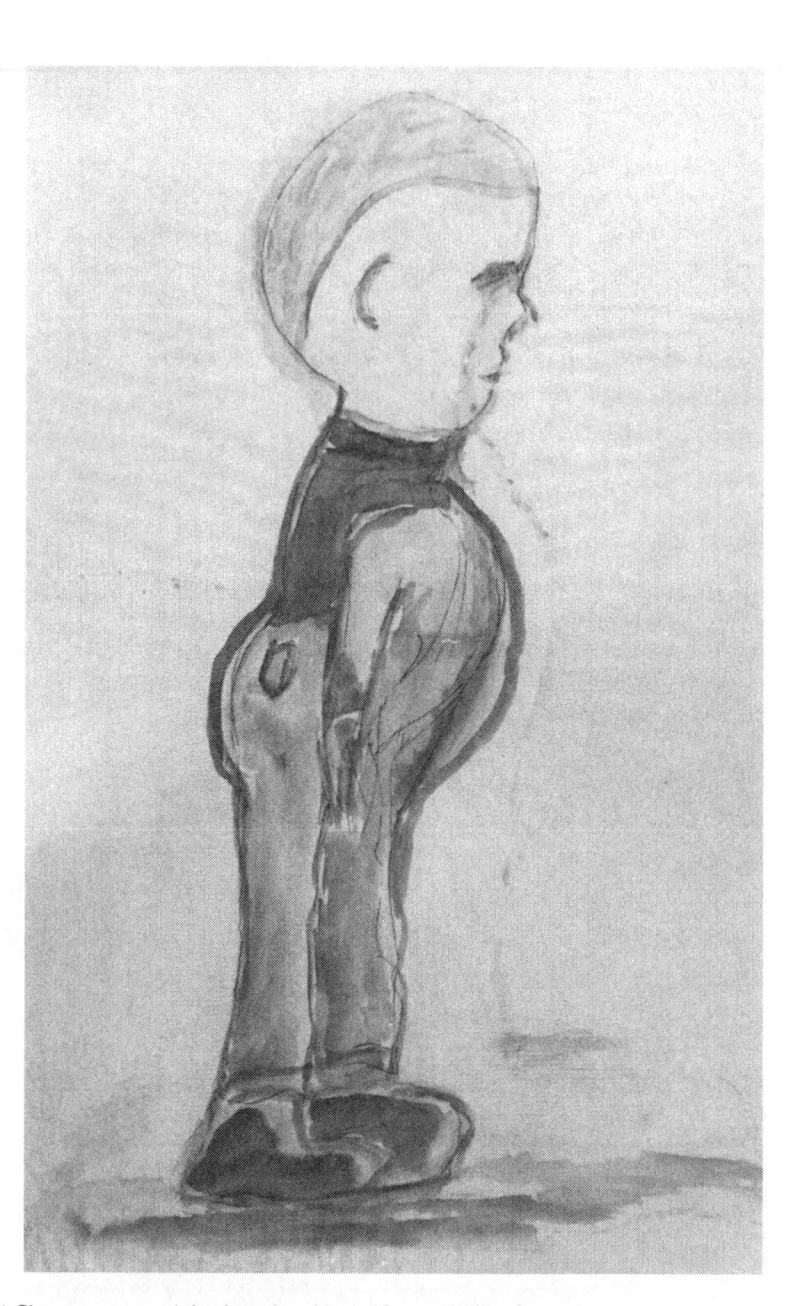

(e) Close to target weight she painted herself in a childlike form with a protruding stomach and crying. She was wearing jeans because she felt at her fattest and most uncomfortable dressed this way. She would be fat, mis-shapen and depressed. Agreeing that the figure looked boy-like she described how she would feel totally unfeminine and unattractive at this weight.

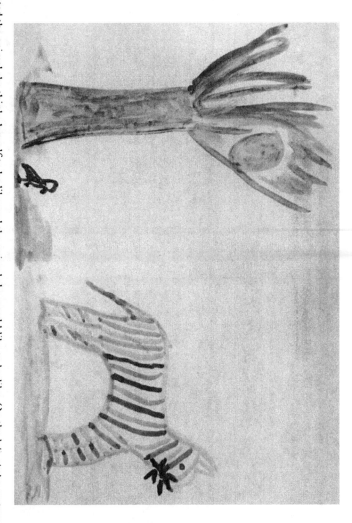

(f) She painted the animal she thinks herself to be like and the animal she would like to be like. On the left of the picture is a rootless tree with a nest in the branches and on the ground is a little bird. The patient herself feels that she has no roots. The bird has either fallen out of the tree or was pushed out—she was not sure which. It has a damaged leg and is hopping along completely by itself having been abandoned by its family. Now that she is well on in treatment she feels that she has been abandoned by her family especially her mother and desperately wants people to care for and about her. On the right of the picture is a tiger which for her represents strength, independence and assertiveness. She agreed that she had also managed to convey the animal as having an air of friendliness and warmth, qualities which she also would have liked to possess.

(g) Asked to paint the future she sketched it as a garden full of trees and pretty colourful flowers but with no people. In the foreground is a wall which she still has to get through before she can reach the garden. There has been a series of walls to get through and this is the last one. She has found it a long and exhausting struggle achieving target weight and she feels that she needs a rest before tackling this next obstacle. However she feels some hope about the future and expects to get into the garden and to find it peopled.

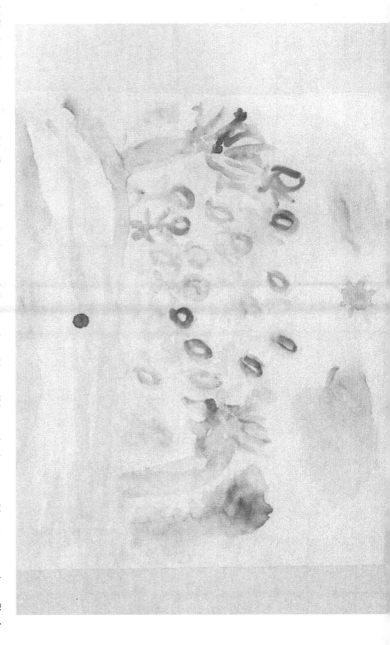

(h) She has been at target weight for several weeks, is up and about and working well in psychotherapy and in group meetings. She has made friends with a number of staff. She now sees herself (the small black spot) as detached from her family (compare with (a)). Many happy people are playing in the area between the trees. She is not part of them but she can see them and may join them.

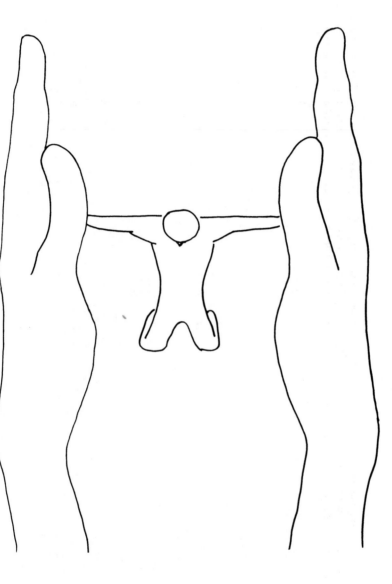

FIG. 20 a–i. This sequence of nine drawings was done by a male anorectic during in-patient treatment. During this period he was involved in individual and family psychotherapy and during the first twelve weeks his weight rose from about 38 to 58 kg (his target weight).

(a) He described this as pressure, which could be seen as pressure from his parents, or from the staff. He described it as a time when he was feeling controlled and pressurized and a feeling that he was being crushed. This painting facilitated early transference interpretations.

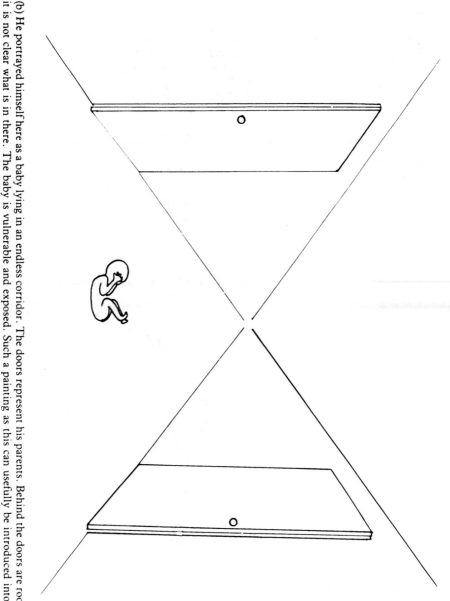

(b) He portrayed himself here as a baby lying in an endless corridor. The doors represent his parents. Behind the doors are rooms but it is not clear what is in there. The baby is vulnerable and exposed. Such a painting as this can usefully be introduced into family therapy.

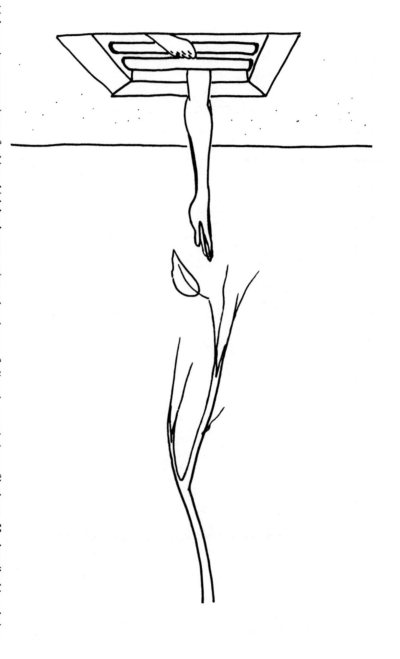

(c) A very important picture for him which he drew at a time when he was feeling the restrictions of bed rest. He described it as being confined to being ill, whilst the leaf on an otherwise barren tree, represented life. Whilst he could reach out nothing could get into him because he was behind bars and because the window was high up. He felt removed and distant—out of touch with reality. At this stage he was still intellectualizing and resisting the friendly availability of the staff.

(d) In this picture the hand has broken the chain. The hand is his. The chain represents bonds and locks, such as those which an escapologist would break free of. It probably represents his anorexia nervosa. He likened his open hand to the marshal arts in which the open hand is seen as being stronger than the closed one. By this stage he was beginning to talk about the violence within him and the damage this could cause others. He was also beginning to befriend the student nurses, in particular, showing an interest in their goals and hopes and talking much more about himself. The specific psychotherapeutic relationships were also much better.

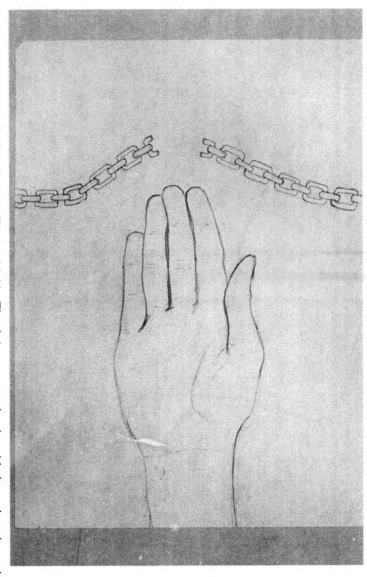

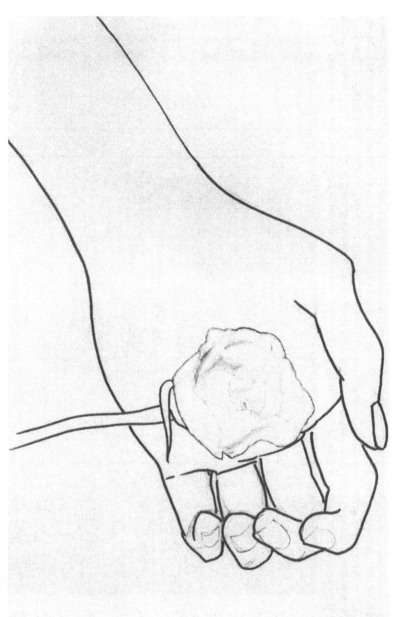

(e) The ambiguous hand. He drew it as his own hand protecting the rose but he agreed that it could also be seen as a hand about to crush it. The rose which is still quite fresh represents life. He had now settled down well in the unit and thought there was a real possibility that he could grow in personality.

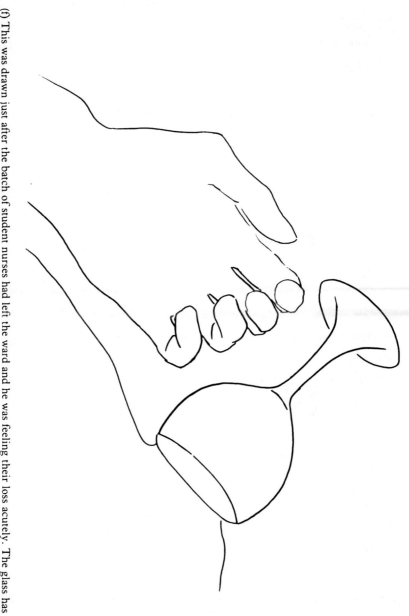

(f) This was drawn just after the batch of student nurses had left the ward and he was feeling their loss acutely. The glass has fallen out of his hand and the red wine has been irrevocably spilled.

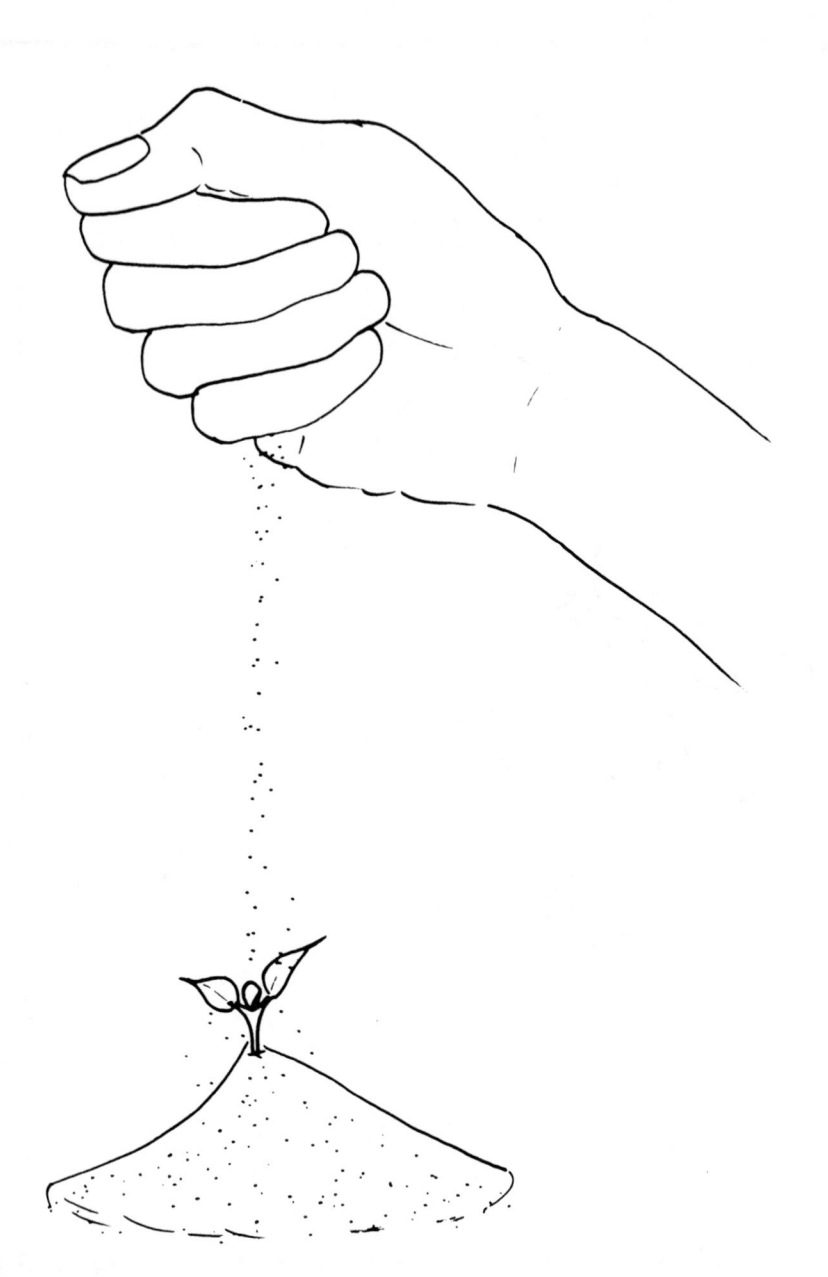

(g) The hour glass. The sand is time, the hand is fate and the small shoot is himself. It is being stifled by the sand which is falling from the hand. He saw himself at this time when he was approaching target weight, as having no control over his destiny so that he felt helpless because nothing he could do would have any effect.

(h) A week or so later and still assailed by doubt he drew this picture which shows a weapon and a baby's rattle connected by a vine. At this stage he had rebelled against the treatment programme, for childish reasons he said. He was not ready for the things for which he was rebelling, i.e. greater freedom. He described the weapon as dangerous but particularly frightening in the hands of a child. The weapon and the rattle are in the grip of the vine which again he begins to feel represent both his parents and the staff.

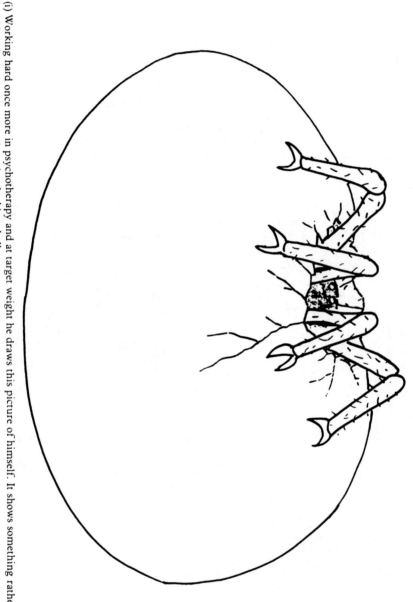

(i) Working hard once more in psychotherapy and at target weight he draws this picture of himself. It shows something rather nasty breaking through a nice clean harmless looking shell.

Formal Psychotherapy

The basis of all psychotherapy is to create a new kind of relationship and thence also other relationships through the contact between the patient and the therapist.

The ongoing relationship with nursing and other staff already described can very importantly provide new experiences for the anorectic, freeing and enabling her to reflect on herself and consider alternative ways of relating to others and alternative attitudes.

An important mechanism operating here is for such staff to resist becoming ensnared in the anorectic's (and her family's) inevitable tendency (which can sometimes too glibly be construed and dismissed as mere manipulation) to incorporate them all into their own established and (so far as the present problem is concerned) faulty way of life. For this not to happen staff require an element of self-awareness at least collectively that is relevant to the anorectic's problems and the latter's impact on them and which must transcend the anorectic's understanding and approach to these matters in the first instance. They need to be able to respond thoughtfully, non-judgementally, but with care and firmness when relevant.

This can best be facilitated in general if it is mirrored in the individual formal psychotherapy in which the anorectic is engaged. The latter is likely to arise on a once or twice-weekly regular basis and last say 50 minutes on each occasion. Simply providing such a relationship can be therapeutic in the way outlined above. However, within it much more can then go on and can be encouraged to go on. The therapist must be prepared for the anorectic to become more psychologically dependent in the first instance if she has indeed, even temporarily, shed her old ways of dealing with people. At the same time she may benefit from frequent reminders that she is dealing with new people and that she should be wary of investing them with images from her past and present family life. Thus such stark and early transference interpretations can continue to be very helpful, freeing communication. At the same time an element of psychological regression is inevitable and to be encouraged, and allows her to begin to share her feelings with the therapist as they continue to explore the background. Sharing of feelings is a crucial step in psychotherapy. For it to happen it is axiomatic that the therapist be capable of the same feelings and of acknowledging them, and even, potentially, of thereby accepting occasional change and development in himself.

One way of adopting new attitudes, especially in someone as psychologically receptive as the anorectic may by now be within the therapeutic situation, is through the process of incorporating those exhibited by others for whom there is an element of high regard, whether this latter be realistic or not. At this stage anorectics may begin tentatively to adopt and try out the new attitudes and behaviour of those around them.

Such developments can be reinforced by (i) social skills training. The majority of anorectics are socially incompetent and can benefit from formalized sessions of role-playing which demand social skills (both this and the re-exposure to normal adult weight which is in process can be regarded as specifically behavioural aspects of the total treatment programme). (ii) Interpretations within the formal psychotherapy. These are statements inviting the patient to consider the possibility of meaningful links suggested as existing between aspects of past and present behaviour and experience of herself and those around her. This sometimes allows the person thereafter to be more reflective in the future, more reflective when otherwise prone to act in habitual and unthinking ways.

In attempting to foster within the patient such personal growth and experience of new ways of coping, there is the likelihood that this will divorce them more from their old relationships. Whereas parents and others may initially be pleased to see such development within the patient away from anorexia nervosa, in the long term they will need to adjust to such changes. In the classical situation it is important to involve the parents at this early stage in similar psychotherapy to that being experienced by the anorectic. Resistances will have to be tackled. In order to try and understand parental attitudes it is necessary now to learn more about their individual backgrounds—experiences which they may never have shared with each other and which are likely therefore to be especially relevant to the present situation.

As with individual therapy the parents can best be helped by a competent psychotherapeutic approach, the relationship aspect of which contains the seeds of change in it for them as well. They will usually meet with two members of staff, e.g. a male doctor and a female social worker, a female doctor and a male nurse.

At some stage within the in-patient programme that will vary from case to case, it will usually become appropriate to meet in family therapy with parents, the patient and sometimes other brothers and sisters all together.

Such meetings are designed (i) to allow a wider sharing of feelings, (ii) concurrently to allow a wider sharing of experiences, e.g. for the mother to be able now to discuss her own adolescent experience and to be able to accept similar information from her daughter, (iii) to examine the pattern of development within the family, often selectively focussing on particular problems which illuminate it and which can be seen as points of departure, for instance the death of one of the parents, or other siblings leaving home, or the start of the patient's menstruation, or the identification of the patient in everyone's mind with one or other parent's own atittudes and nature. The aim must be for habitual transactions within the family such as blaming, avoiding, placating, smothering and preaching to be examined within the ambience of such therapy. Individuals can learn, and can be seen by other family members to learn, for the first time the effects that they have on other members. This enables scrutiny of the basis for such attitudes. Family members must begin to test each other out more and take risks, without which growth cannot occur. Insight can be acquired through interpretation, for instance the early interpretation of the transference within individual psychotherapy already referred to, and can also arise retrospectively from new vantage points of personal and family growth.

When the anorectic has gained weight these ongoing approaches can be supplemented with small-group psychotherapy. Here the patient begins to share her problems with fellow patients in a formal and supervised way and to assume some responsibility for beginning to help others with their problems. This may be very difficult for her but the experience of being in such a group, even if she remains essentially a silent member, can still be helpful. Indeed, such difficulty is realistic and is to be preferred to the opposite tendency which can arise wherein the individual gratuitously and dominatingly insists on trying to solve other people's problems to the exclusion of her own. Such people are sometimes also wont, unwisely and precipitately, to wish to train in one of the caring professions. For an anorectic who has just got her weight back and who is in a state of experiential turmoil and uncertainty, no precipitate decisions should be endorsed concerning such matters as careers. Some anorectics can also be helped at this stage by involvement in a closed "trust" group which runs for about six to eight weeks. Within this, role playing, often within the context of family sculpting, is encouraged. Complementing this arousal by role play is a search for the experience of feelings through bodily activity. This physical activity includes dancing, vigorous exercise and the touching of others.

Figure 17 (a–e) (see p. 107–109) shows the kinds of weight change that typically occur within this in-patient programme. The charts show the associated kindling of pubertal hormonal processes, all of which the patient is now having to come to terms with.

Conscious attempts to bring about the psychological changes outlined above in the anorectic and her family generate, if they are at all effective, certain consequences.

The anorectic and her parents may all begin to feel uncertain about themselves and each other. This needs to be recognized and respected for the strain it is. They will need to continue to tolerate such uncertainty for some time yet and they may be less equipped than most to do this.

Such strains may reveal themselves in specific ways, crystallizing out for instance as depression, weight change or a precipitation of physical illness in the parents; depression, panic or impulsive behaviour in the patient.

Depression, meaning the experience and recognition of hopelessness and despair together with a new sense of loneliness, can, at least at times, be a positive force—reflecting reality and recognition of the actual changes that still need to occur. In the author's view "disease" of many kinds is sometimes an alternative and more primitive (i.e. unrealistic and avoidance-based) response. To experience depression and cope with it may be the price of recovery for the anorectic. She may, of course, have been depressed within her illness. However, her new depression is different, as discussed earlier in the book.

Psychological treatment of such depression requires extra time, sometimes best spent within an extension of in-patient care. Antidepressant drugs at this stage are rarely helpful. Instead, both the patient, her family and the therapists need to review the situation systematically. The anorectic, now no longer starved and struggling instead to maintain what others claim is a normal body shape, is at last and once again in touch with her more natural psychological self. Exploration of this will allow further clarification of the despair, revelation of potential narcissism, grandiosity, self-destructive propensities, which can begin to be understood to some extent in terms of the family system as well as the anorectic's own needs. Parents may need to become newly involved with these aspects of themselves in order to support the patient. Other anorectics may show a more integrated self at this stage, reflected in more understandable neurotic reality-related social anxieties.

Another risk in all of this is that the anorectic will retrench—revert to old ways in the face of so much distress. Hints that this is about to happen include her mounting blandness and her increasing tendency to split staff members into being "good" or "bad". Even when this happens, in the author's experience, the anorectic concerned can still sometimes recover some while later but using the experiences gained whilst in the hospital to help her in this.

The period of in-patient stay comes towards its end with the patient now usually going home, for instance at weekends. She will have become very used to the hospital programme of eating and will be frightened that some new menus will deviate from what is intended by the treatment programme. Her parents will be equally apprehensive. It is well for her to go home with clear ideas about the nature of meals during the first few weeks. Nursing staff, occupational therapy staff or dieticians will by now have met with the families and planned out menus within reasonable limits. The anorectic often gets important reassurance from such a plan, which she sees as due recognition of this major transitional difficulty.

The problem in any health service is to provide as intensive care as is needed. For instance, resources only allow one or two sessions of psychotherapy a week even within the most intensive part of the programme. This can be complemented to some extent by the knowledge that someone is always potentially available in a moment of crisis. After discharge from hospital there are even greater problems. If the patient is to struggle on (I call her a patient now to allow her to be one and yet also to consider being ex-anorectic) she must not feel abandoned. The temptation to revert to severe anorexia nervosa is now many times greater than was the case when she was in hospital. Weekly or bi-weekly psychotherapy should continue for at least a year and more often for two or three years. The family will need to remain in meaningful and often regular predictable contact, usually through the social worker. For it is during these times that the potential arises for more insightful understanding within the family and the patient. As they experience this retrospective insight, achieved through their new risk taking, explorations and personal developments, they will especially benefit from proper concern, support and clarification of what is happening and its consequences. Now is the time when new, more solid options are arising and when healthy discussions are important for a growing sense of autonomy (Fig. 21).

This struggle, in which the person escaping from anorexia nervosa is involved over the first year or two of such treatment, is at times immense and overwhelming. It must be remembered that approximately 40% of severely ill anorectics can expect to have "recovered" naturally or else be "very much improved" after about six years. However with treatment, in my view, not only will people such as these have been helped to a more rapid and substantial improvement but about half of the remainder will also be "recovered" or very nearly so. Thus overall 70–80% will be much better. The lack of precision evident in these figures arises not least because of the variations in recovery in respect of different aspects of the disorder. Thus 70% of females will have some degree of menstrual activity including periods: the majority of them will have regular periods. Over 60% will have a normal and stable body weight and nearly another

FIG. 21. Treatment aims expressed diagrammatically for someone who fell ill at the age of 18, height 5 ft 3 in (160 cms) and who presents for treatment, aged 21. 1. Restoration of body weight to neutral level in terms of comparability with a non-anorectic general population of similar height and age at which the individual developed anorexia nervosa, leading to re-exposure to reality of shape-related conflicts. 2. Resolution of these conflicts through development of (a) alternative solutions within family, and (b) greater and other coping resources within the individual.

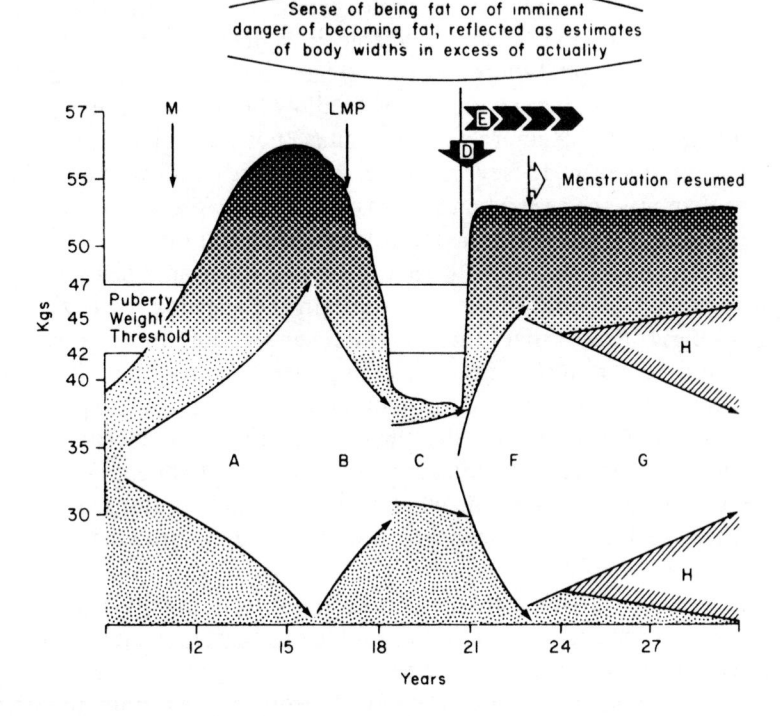

Code A. Mounting adolescent turmoil, increasingly construed in terms of body shape. B. Resolution of this turmoil as anorexia nervosa develops. C. Social conflict now avoided but fear of fatness persists because of constant threat of loss of control over eating and consequent weight gain. Meanwhile psychosocial maturation is impossible. D. Body weight change during in-patient treatment. E. Input of psychotherapy with family and patient. F. Rekindling of adolescent conflict over shape. G. Slowly reducing concern over shape. Increasing sense of ownership of body. H. Growing capacity to handle adolescent problems in terms other than shape, and increasing experience of mastery over own adult destiny.

20% will be approaching this (Fig. 22). Many will still worry about their shape but not all to the same degree as before and probably in a way that also characterizes many other women who have never had the condition. In terms of social and sexual adjustment perhaps 60–70% will have fulfilment of a kind comparable with others who have not had the condition. Moreover, fewer will be dead than would otherwise have been the case.

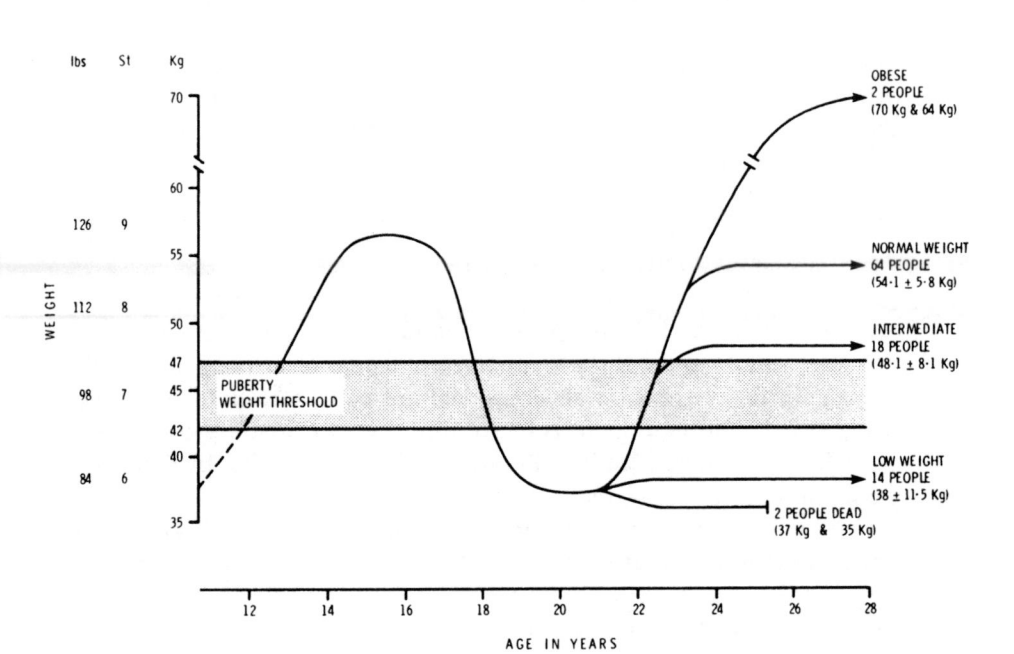

FIG. 22. This chart shows the outcome in respect of body weight of a group of severely ill anorectics who have engaged in extensive treatment of the kind described in this book. Although the majority have a body weight within 12% of normal, only 55 were judged to be truly recovered in all respects. Thus the remainder of those with normal weight still experienced menstrual irregularities, still experienced excessive concern over their shape, and felt themselves to be grappling with major psychosocial problems. Fourteen per cent remained severely ill. Two patients had died, fewer than would probably have been the case had there been no treatment. Two had become very obese, i.e. there are now fewer obese people in this population than one would find in the general population.

Alternative Developments

The above has been an account of one treatment approach (mine and my team's) to the classic case—a young female patient and her parents all involved in in-patient care. There are many exceptions to this. For instance:

1. The Anorectic and her Family who Decide *not* to Accept the Offer of In-patient Treatment (the majority offered it do accept it)

Sometimes the need not to interrupt studies is advanced as reason for not wishing to enter hospital. This and less seemingly important issues are likely to reflect the anorectic's and her family's ambivalence about admission. They can also reflect the alarm of parents that education may be interrupted—of course dedication to academic work may be an important ingredient of the anorexia nervosa itself and also reflect forces within the family contributing to its onset.

If the offer to arrange education in hospital is not acceptable then my practice is to discuss fully the possible reasons for such an attitude and to offer to continue to see the patient and her family or arrange for this to happen within the unit on an occasional out-patient basis for the time being, say for the nine months or so until the exmainations have been taken. The patient and family will probably be insisting that by that time she will anyway be recovered.

They will be told that, at the end of this period, we can all assess the situation again. If the patient is still "ill" (as is most often the case) then a further offer of treatment on an in-patient basis is likely to be made. If they reject this, then further discussion will occur regarding the desirability and acceptability of referral back to the family doctor or other referring source. Alternatively attempts to help, still using the unit's special expertise on an out-patient basis, may again be made. However, if in-patient care has been advocated in the first instance as a necessary basis for further treatment, then the decision later to offer treatment instead solely on an out-patient basis is rarely made since this latter approach alone will already have been judged as unprofitable. Under these circumstances the anorectic and the family is better off knowing the limits of help available from any one source.

2. The Anorectic who Enters In-patient Treatment without her Parents from whom she may be Estranged or who may not be Available

The treatment approach here is no different in principle and clearly is focussed more on the patient herself. Under these circumstances it is often profitable, with the patient's agreement, to involve any important friends who are willing to become so engaged.

3. The Married Anorectic

As stated earlier in the book, an anorectic who has married may have consolidated her illness thereby, since its existence may be crucial to the stability of the new relationship. Nevertheless her presence as a patient reflects some urge either on her part or her husband's part (or rarely his part or his wife's part if the patient is male) to change.

If the spouse is seeking change in her this is promising since she may now herself need to change in order to maintain the relationship. However she may remain torn between conflicting loyalties, say to her husband and to others such as her parents. In such cases parents, for instance, may also profitably be involved in treatment.

If however the motivation to change is mainly hers then there may be resistance from him to this whole idea of treatment aimed at facilitating such change. For instance such marriages may be unconsummated or barely so. The patient may be well aware that her husband has no knowledge of the "other side of her nature" which she nevertheless suspects will again be released once her weight and hormonal status are returned to normal. He only knows her as the child that she once was; not as the adolescent she had temporarily become before the "illness" developed.

Under such circumstances it is obviously important to try to help the husband to become involved and to engage in psychotherapy without impairing his self-esteem.

The outcome of such treatment, if it is successful with the patient, can nevertheless sometimes lead to a break-up of such marriages. Alternatively, in some instances of anorexia nervosa within a marriage the basic psychopathology appears not so much to be related to the need for suppression of one side of the anorectic's general nature, albeit an impulse ridden aspect, as to a very specific sexual conflict, often seemingly of an incestuous kind. The anorexia nervosa comes on or recurs in the time following pregnancy and childbirth when deep shame is experienced at residual weight gain following the pregnancy. Such conflicts importantly transcend the marriage and often require more intense individual therapy, though marital therapy remains important.

4. The Marginally Ill Anorectic, or the Anorectic Close to Recovery

Such anorectics can be helped with out-patient treatment alone although it can be a serious mistake to believe that the anorectic is marginally ill merely because her weight is not severely reduced. Anorexia nervosa can be very firmly established at a weight of say 43 kgs for the reasons advanced earlier in this book.

5. The Chronically Ill Anorectic

Some such anorectics become caught up in potential treatment pro-grammes often 20 or more years after the onset of their illness. They are particularly likely to be unable to cope with the implications and experience of major weight gain back to adult proportions. Any injudicious shift of their low weight control mechanisms may precipitate them into intense panic and disgust; even too provocative exploration with them of the psychopathology underlying their condition can have the same effect. Suicide is then a danger. Such matters must be fully explored together with such an anorectic. On the other hand this kind of person is often, at this stage, without further resource as an anorectic. She may be isolated, deeply despairing within herself, dangerously low in body weight and on the brink of physical collapse.

A joint agreed goal not to banish the anorexia nervosa but instead to attempt to stabilize it at a level more compatible with survival and the capacity to be active and more independent may be the best approach.

Such a limited explicit contract offered by the therapist, a statement that he agrees that the patient is probably better off, all things considered, remaining anorectic, can be most helpful and often a totally new experience for the anorectic. She can approach the task of limited weight gain with much more confidence under such circumstances. However, without doubt, she will remain severely impaired in a physical, psycho-logical and social sense, and her condition will continue to carry a high risk of early death. In some, the healing effects of time may also eventually arise, as has been described in detail in Chapter 3.

12
The Rights of the "Patient"

The title of this book is intended to express an aspect of this matter. I have suggested all along that anorexia nervosa is a response to, a profound retreat from and avoidance of, the struggle to be an adult individual acceptable to themselves and those around them. The anorectic, through her nature, and her experiences, has been unable to secure the right to be healthily independent i.e. mature. Now, with her anorexia nervosa, she finds many would also deny her the right to stay as she is. They are worried about her present state, they cannot understand it, they (the family, doctors, etc.) feel that it is an indictment of themselves.

Does a person with anorexia nervosa now have "the right" to change, either in isolation from her family or together with them; alternatively, does she have "the right" to stay as she is?

How does the would-be therapist, intent on "getting her better" through what can easily come to be seen as an imposed treatment programme, escape the paradox that he thereby becomes yet one more person denying her the right to exercise and develop her own "self"? My own attempts to solve this dilemma have been outlined in the previous chapter and the rationale for this in earlier chapters. It has involved the removal of the patient's control over her own body weight, the restoration of this to normal levels, the inevitable confrontation with the reality of adolescent struggle which this provokes, and the attempts therein to provide a new *freedom* to explore herself as a person. This attempt, to disengage the anorectic conceptually from domination by her body weight, does not by any means always succeed. Therefore should the person trying to help routinely engage instead in treatment of a more flexible kind taking much more into account the anorectic's current needs? In our present state of understanding of the condition—which is limited—my answer is No. I believe I have encountered many anorectics who have gained in psychological strength from being enabled to engage

in treatment on the terms described in the previous chapter. But by
enablement here is meant that *they have decided to do so.* What of the
anorectic who decides not to do so? Some such instances have been
outlined, again in the previous chapter. Beyond this, it is probably
important for the anorectic to recognize that there are definite limits to
the help available. Given the extent of the problem within the population,
specialized treatment resources in particular should be preserved for
those who, given preliminary help, eventually choose to engage in such
treatment.

But the anorectic also has the *right* to be helped to survive with her
illness. Since maintaining a low and immature body weight is a biologically unstable condition, the task of attempting to bring some element of
stability to such a state is profoundly challenging and requires an
appreciation of both the physical and experiential elements contained
within it. An analogy might be the right given to opiate addicts to be
maintained in a statutorily acceptable way by medically optimal
prescription of their addictive drugs.

Can compulsory detention ever be justified in anorexia nervosa. In
these islands the Mental Health Act of 1959 allows compulsory detention,
care and sometimes relevant emergency treatment of persons judged to
be in imminent danger of harming themselves and resistant to such help.
Application for such detention and care usually needs to be made by the
nearest relative or otherwise a social worker. I have inevitably found
myself involved in such clinical issues from time to time.

The routine response of anorectics to the offer of treatment is to refuse
it. Within the approach outlined and advocated in this book this still
sometimes happens.

The acute danger envisaged by those around such a severely ill
anorectic may either be (i) that they are severely emaciated, metabolically
deranged and perceptually disturbed so as to be unaware of their extreme
physical condition and imminent death—they may still see themselves as
reasonably nourished or claim this to be so; or more fundamentally and
secretly still be terrified of the prospect of the tiniest weight gain—
something which they may now recognize themselves as very prone to
since they are likely to be dehydrated and liable to water retention given
any fluid intake; (ii) that they are suicidal.

If terminal inanition associated with resistance to treatment is seen as a
medical problem, then should the anorectic have the right to die?
Patients with other mortal conditions such as cancer, refusing treatment
that might save their lives, cannot be compelled to undergo such

treatment even if their decision is rooted in misconception. Only if they were also severely depressed and the judgement made that their thinking was a product of such depression, might compulsory detention be a possible statutory course of action. It would still not be possible to treat the physical illness—merely the depression. In the case of the anorectic can their extreme condition and current deterioration be seen as a kind of suicide? Can their inability to recognize their state or at least to acknowledge it to others be construed as a perceptual disorder of psychotic proportions. More fundamentally, even if detained, can the course of the disorder and such states of mind change. In my view they can. I have occasionally recommended detention under such conditions and am certain that the patients would otherwise have died. In the event I can think of several such patients who have subsequently fully recovered from the condition and are now pleased to be alive. However, what about the situation of imminent suicidal intent.

Such intent may or may not be superficially evident. The anorectic may quite clearly be in a state of terminal existential despair or she may be bland, hostile and denying any suicidal intent. Compulsory detention and care can often be seen within routine psychiatric practice as within acceptable limits under such circumstances. However, one can rarely hope to achieve anything other than a temporary amelioration of the crisis by such a step. The *compulsory* patient has got to be helped to become a *voluntary* patient at the very earliest opportunity if some greater impact on the course of events is sought.

Over the last 20 years I have been involved in the treatment of over 400 anorectics, most of them severely ill and often in crisis. I have made the decision to compulsorily detain such patients on about half a dozen occasions. On each occasion I have found myself in touch with the heart of the matter of anorexia nervosa and its treatment.

13
Self-help Techniques

If it is true that intervention in anorexia nervosa cannot be effective in terms of curing the disorder unless the individual wants help and strives to help herself within the treatment, then can so-called self-help techniques themselves benefit the person with anorexia nervosa and/or her family who are determined not to consult the doctor. Such attempts at self-help take two main forms: (i) personal efforts, (ii) lay support and counselling organizations. The element of self-help in the latter rests in the ability of the individual to decide to join such a group and the resources such a group can then provide to further enable the individual concerned to help herself.

Personal Efforts

The anorectic will need to obtain more information about anorexia nervosa in general in the first instance. A number of books have been written on the subject suitable for such a purpose and they are listed at the end of this chapter. Through such reading she may come to learn more about herself and, at the least, her motivation to change may be increased. The same will apply to her family.

Support and Counselling Organizations and Services

Anorexia nervosa is one of many conditions recognized by some of those with it or concerned about it as requiring understanding in social and psychological terms as well as physical ones, and inviting the development of non-medical self-help groups. Such groups exist in widespread fashion now for such conditions as alcoholism, drug dependence, obesity, agoraphobia and depression. Sometimes they arise also in relation to the needs of the families. Anorexia nervosa is one condition where the families often wish there were some such support.

Many support groups operate on the principle that those joining them must wish to be rid of their disorder; sometimes membership is contingent on this. Such groups are often run by people recently recovered from the condition. Problems here arise since many people recovered from such conditions prefer to put the whole matter behind them. The last thing they wish is to remain involved with present day sufferers. Sometimes, as everyone in a caring profession should know, those who set themselves up to help others may be anxiously fending off the disorder in themselves. Such motivation need not be destructive to those with the disorder providing it is recognized, but such recognition may undermine the capacity of the would-be helper.

There are several organizations in Britain* currently concerned with self-help techniques for anorexia nervosa (e.g. Anorexic Aid, The Priory Centre, 11 Priory Road, High Wycombe, Bucks). Their aims are practical ones of befriending the isolated anorectic, providing support and guidance to families and friends, providing an opportunity for the individual with anorexia nervosa to make contact with others who have similar problems, providing group counselling and providing channels through which more expert individual counselling can be sought. The organizations work through a network of local groups linked by occasional general meetings and a newsletter. That some anorectics derive help from such systems is undoubted although, inevitably, anorectics motivated to seek such help are also likely to be those approaching the time when they can anyway contemplate change. In my view such groups, comprising mainly recovered anorectics, can, if competently run, be helpful and there can be mutual benefit to all concerned if they have links with professional services, medical and social.

Within the USA* too there are now a number of organizations concerned with self-help and with facilitating help (e.g. Anorexia Nervosa Aid Inc., 101 Cedar Lane, Teaneck, New Jersey 07666; Anorexia Nervosa Aid Society of Massachusetts Inc., Sandy Road, Lincoln, Massachusetts 01773). Thus these agencies, apparently involving many in their administration who have never had the disorder, strive to occupy middle ground between the anorectic and caring professionals. They encourage self-help groups, act as referral agencies to psychiatrists and others known to be interested and rated as effective. They organize conferences and lectures and seek publicity through newspapers, handouts and public talks to high school groups, school nurses, teachers. Some are apparently available also as an emergency service along Samaritan lines. They recognize as important the problems facing the anorectic attempting to rehabilitate herself in a strange and threatening larger world. The best of such developments as these again command the author's respect, since he believes them sometimes to be effective in their goals.

*In the last few years a number of additional self-help groups have sprung up. The author maintains an up to date list of groups in the United Kingdom, North America and elsewhere which have indicated their willingness to be included. This list can be made available to interested people who should then write to him at the following address: Academic Department of Psychiatry, St. George's Hospital Medical School, Cranmer Terrace, London SW17 0RE, (U.K.) enclosing a stamped addressed envelope or international reply coupon.

Other Reading

Bruch, H. (1974) *Eating Disorders*. London: Routledge & Kegan Paul.

Bruch, H. (1978) *The Golden Cage*. London: Open Books.

Dally, P., Gomez, J. and Isaacs, A. J. (1979) *Anorexia Nervosa*. London: Heinemann.

Kaufman, M. R. *et al*. (1964) *Evolution of Psychosomatic Concepts*. Anorexia Nervosa: A Paradigm. London: Hogarth.

Lambley, P. (1983) *How to Survive Anorexia Nervosa*. London: Muller.

Levenkron, S. (1978) "The Best Little Girl in the World." Chicago: Contemporary Books Inc.

Minuchin, S. *et al*. (1978) *Psychosomatic Families:* Anorexia nervosa in context. Harvard: Harvard University Press.

Palmer, R. L. (1980) Anorexia Nervosa. London: Penguin.

Selvini, M. P. (1974) *Self Starvation*. London: Human Context Books.

Thoma, H. (1967) *Anorexia Nervosa*. New York: International Universities Press.

14
Factors Affecting Outcome

Another strength of the illness model approach to anorexia nervosa is that it sharpens up the capacity to classify aspects of the condition, physical, behavioural, experiential and social, that are associated with a variety of outcomes ranging from recovery through to chronicity and early death. Such analyses are always statistical exercises—they allow one to begin to quantify the chances of a particular outcome actually occurring. Some individual cases will not conform to such generalization, especially in respect of any one variable, and in these instances the prediction has proved totally wrong. This point is laboured here because the following factors as presented should all be considered within its context. No one should despair. I have seen many exceptions in every instance. Many of the effects are related to each other, and the findings only apply to that group of anorectics who have been studied so far within the medical system, and in particular within the author's and one or two other worker's own clinical experience.

Underlying Personality Potential

Anorexia nervosa arises on the brink of adolescent personality formation and is a massive retreat from this challenge. Only when weight is again normal are the anorectic's potential personality resources again generated and expressed. Clearly present age and age of onset, both chronological and biological (i.e. related to age of puberty), need to be taken into account in making any such evaluation. Rekindled and intensified personality traits of the "borderline" kind, e.g. impulsivity especially in respect of sexual behaviour, chronic anger, empty depression, grandiosity, narcissism, friendlessness, self- destructiveness, a tendency to

massive splitting of other people into crude categories of good and bad
and to other indiscriminatory behaviour, all reflect a greater psychological maturational task confronting the individual, and make it the
more likely that primitive protective avoidance responses such as the
retreat into anorexia nervosa will recur.

Gender

It used to be thought that male anorectics, at least those reaching the clinic,
were less likely to recover from their disorder than females. Perhaps only the
most severely afflicted were referred. Thus male anorectics may be even more
successful than females at concealing their disorder from others. Male clothing
covers up the emaciated figure. A thin male is likely to be accepted by his peers
as unusual but they are probably less likely to recognize that the thinness is a
function of overwhelming concern about body shape than is the thin female's
peer group. Then again, excessive eating and vomiting are more acceptable cul-
turally in at least some male circles.

In fact, the remarkable thing about male anorexia nervosa is how similar it
is to that in the female. Differences between the sexes are minimized by the
condition. Recently it has become evident that males have a similar prognosis
to females with individual outlook also being governed by similar factors. Adolescent males, though less prone to anorexia nervosa than females, are of
course more likely than females to develop other kinds of morbidity such as
delinquency or drug dependence.

Social Class

The relationship of this factor to outcome may now be changing since the
distribution of the disorder within society appears to be changing.
However, over the past 20 years, the condition has definitely been more
common in middle class families than working class families. Individuals
with anorexia nervosa coming from this latter background had, in
general, a lesser chance of recovery than others. It may be that, in the
past, the working class environment and related attitudes have exercised
a protective effect in relation to all but the most vulnerable of potential
anorectics amongst them.

Major Premorbid Obesity

This is more often associated with a deep fear within the anorectic of reversion to obesity and a tendency to overeat leading to frequent vomiting and purging as the means of maintaining low body weight.

Regular and Frequent Overeating/Vomiting /Purging

This pattern leads to a less stable low body weight, itself engendering even more alarm over potential unavoidable major weight gain and thence even more intensive food avoidance/vomiting etc. In addition, the general physical health of such a person steadily becomes severely impaired. Such dietary patterns often arise some years after the onset of the disorder and are probably more common in the previously obese, and are often associated with more rigid parental character structures.

Chronicity

The longer the person has been ill e.g. 12 years compared with four years, the more difficult it is to recover and the less likely.

Age of Onset

The earlier the onset following the start of puberty the better the outcome. Such cases often present early on in the development of the disorder and perhaps represent a greater proportion of the total number of cases than is so amongst those in whom the age of onset is later. The latter may for instance develop the condition away from home and family pressures for them to seek treatment. Thus forms destined to be milder may present to doctors from amongst those in whom the condition has arisen early in life.

Pervasive Despair and Hopelessness

Though this is experienced by all anorectics, some experience it only transitorily. If present both at low and normal body weight as the dominating state of mind then there is less chance of complete recovery. This should not be confused with the proper and evident distress following restoration of body weight to normal within in-patient treatment as described earlier, which is associated with a better long term outlook.

Lack of Motivation to Change, Whether Through Despair or Overriding Panic

This point has been frequently emphasized within the book. It is the would-be therapist's task to unearth and facilitate motivation to change and only to judge its lack within such optimal conditions.

Poor Social Adjustment in Childhood

The inability to secure even childhood friendships now bodes less well for recovery.

Parental Neurotic and Affective Disorder

Sustained anxiety, neurotic avoidance patterns and vulnerability to depression in the parents confers a worse outlook on the anorectic.

Parental Marital Discord

Major conflict between the parents whether or not precipitated out in terms of separation, and

Rigidity in Parents Especially the Father

Fixed attitudes in the parents, hostility to change and sustained denial of problems and of conflict, often reflected in an inability to become involved within treatment of the kind described here, bode ill.

It is, of course, fair enough for researchers to tease out these factors in statistical exercises, but people with anorexia nervosa can take heart from the sure knowledge that as individuals we have much in common with each other but also always characteristics that are unique. It is not possible for any one of us, however experienced, to predict in a completely accurate way how an anorectic will do. It is anorexia nervosa which, beneath the bravure, effectively reduces people to being less than themselves due to the dominating influences of starvation on the one hand and the always present all-consuming fight to avoid weight gain in the presence of plenty on the other. If one can begin, however slightly and with help if necessary, to shake off this grip, then individuality begins to emerge and the statistics can be challenged. The anorectic may belong to a sub-group which has been identified as having a worse prognosis than others, say with only 30% of people within it recovering fully over five years; nevertheless, for those 30 in every 100 who are going to recover fully within this period the attribution of poor prognosis has proved to be quite wrong.

15

The "Patient" Speaks

What follows is a series of anonymous personal accounts of their experiences by people who have or who have had anorexia nervosa, and there are also four accounts by parents. In some instances the writers have been engaged in treatment not necessarily with the author's team. I would like to express here my gratitude to them for the contributions they have made.

I was nineteen years old when I decided to lose some weight. I was nearing the end of my first year at college where I was training to be an infant teacher. I was very unhappy and depressed and I recall clearly the day I resolved to deal with the situation. I conceded to myself that I would always be unhappy (such was my depression) but that I had two alternatives. The first was to be unhappy and fat, and the second to be unhappy and thin. I opted for the latter.

For many years, through my adolescence and teens, I had been labelled "Tub" by my brother, who would taunt me unmercifully with this nickname. My parents condoned his behaviour, having their own name of "Rhino" for me, on account of my clumsiness. I suppose no malice was intended, but these names hurt during those particularly sensitive years.

I concealed my hurt feelings and rage at being so labelled, but came to be very self-conscious, and to feel that being large or fat was not nice or desirable. This notion was strengthened considerably when at 15 I embarked upon a relationship which was to last four years with a boyfriend who took delight in pointing out and magnifying my physical imperfections once he had discovered this chink in my armour.

And so, at 19, convinced of my unloveliness, I began to shed weight in an effort to change my body.

I was very pleased, when after losing about 14 lbs, I found I was arousing a fair amount of interest amongst my fellow male students. I became much more confident of my abilities to attract the opposite sex, and gain their approval. I found a super new boyfriend and ditched the one who had caused me so much unhappiness, something I thought I would never be able to do. Life went well for a few months. I discovered that my periods had stopped, but strangely this did not worry me unduly. I noticed other changes too. My body hair seemed to grow more slowly, and I didn't sweat very much. I remember being pleased that this meant I no longer had to bother with the nuisance of periods, the removal of unwanted hair, or worry about whether I smelt or not, this being one of my adolescent anxieties.

During the next few months, however, it became much harder to keep to my very strict diet. I was by now eating very little, and was always desperately hungry. Yet I was completely "hooked" onto compulsive slimming. I threw myself into my academic studies, working very hard indeed, and achieved a high standard in all I undertook, in spite of my poor physical condition. I walked everywhere instead of taking the bus in order to burn up as many calories as possible, and did frantic dances in my room to music from my record player.

My teachers and friends were now noticing my extreme thinness, but I would repeatedly deny that I was on any kind of diet or that I was in any way ill, for fear that I would be coaxed or forced to eat properly again, thus regaining my original weight, which to me meant becoming ugly and unloved once more.

All this took place during my second year at college. By the time I was due to return for my third and final year I knew I could no longer go on this way. I was skeletal in appearance, very tired, very depressed and above all, desperately hungry. And yet I was *terrified* of gaining any weight. What was I to do? By a great stroke of luck I consulted my doctor at home concerning the absence of my periods. I was probably prompted to do this by my mother, but I can't quite remember. At first he prescribed the pill to restore and regularize my menstrual cycle, but on second thoughts decided to send me to hospital for tests to check for any physical disorder, before taking further action. He had diagnosed anorexia nervosa.

I began to eat as soon as I was admitted to hospital. In fact I could not stop eating and very rapidly returned to my original weight. Although unable to stop this compulsive eating, I was terrified the whole time of the consequences. Ironically I became far heavier than I had ever been. However, after two years as an outpatient undergoing psychotherapy I made a good recovery. I gained an insight into why I had fallen victim of the condition, which has prevented any serious relapse. I have been *very* happily married for six and a half years and have two fine sons.

———————

For many months before my husband and I received confirmation that our daughter had anorexia I had been feeling helpless in the knowledge that there was something seriously wrong with her; at the back of my mind I thought she had anorexia, which I had heard about and seen in another girl some eight years before. Yet no doctor would diagnose this and we had been passed from one consultant to another over a long period of time. She was getting thinner, more depressed, and was constantly tired, and during this time tension and frustration were growing throughout the family. Because we knew there was something wrong we all tried to keep our emotions away from her but this only served to worsen the atmosphere.

She would never sit down, could not relax, was always on the go, cooking, clearing away the table (often before everyone had finished) and washing up. She was fastidious to an unreasonable degree, not only in her own cleanliness but in everything she did. She had a very high standard and the rest of the family couldn't always live up to it. She lost all confidence in herself, did not go out very often, and if she did it was usually with my husband or myself. She would go to bed at about eight o'clock every evening and would be up at half-past five in the morning. She was careful, almost miserly, with money; she would save up and pay for everything herself, yet when it came to giving presents she was very generous.

She is the middle child and, in fact, had everything going for her; she was good academically and a good athlete, very popular at school, but when she was about 14 our eldest son had problems at his boarding school and was, in fact, asked to leave. He always seemed to create problems over spending pocket money and was very demanding in many ways.

Subsequently, he was accepted into our daughter's local grammar school, in the year above her. He started in the September of his "O" level year, and managed to pass four "O" levels. During this time he was very anti-work and we had constant arguments about the amount he borrowed for the things he wanted —often we thought unreasonably.

Our youngest daughter is very easy going but always took the view that she wasn't very bright and couldn't do things. Our daughter who developed anorexia felt everything rested on her shoulders and that she could not let the family down by failing her own exams. We never pressed any of the children on the question of examinations but think that she felt that her brother had let us down.

Looking back, we were never a family who showed our feelings and love towards our children physically, and when they succeeded in something we probably gave them the feeling that it was in any case expected of them.

I feel that the family therapy sessions which we attended while our daughter was in hospital helped us a lot and made us all sit down to talk about ourselves and our relationships. I feel that the previous lack of this was probably largely responsible for her anorexia. It made us realize that she had been unconsciously wanting attention and was being overshadowed by everyone else's personalities and problems. She related to my husband better than to me because he was the one most like her under these conditions—he steered away from family rows and preferred a quiet life. The remainder of the family is rather volatile. The therapy sessions made us think about each other and the effects that our differing personalities had on each other.

Even though we appear to be over the worst, our daughter still has periods of depression and is still very careful about what she eats. We try to say nothing about this as I feel she is well aware of what she is doing and is still touchy about the subject. We had a difficult period when my youngest daughter's boyfriend was killed in a car accident and I felt at the time that my elder daughter didn't like all the attention going to the youngest—in fact, there came a point when I shrieked at her and told her to shut up. I immediately realized that for at least two years that sort of emotion had been very carefully controlled between us and

I felt the shrieking did a lot of good. I feel that she won't be truly happy until she has sorted out her career.

About six months after leaving hospital she seemed to be getting depressed again but after reading books on human sexual behaviour there was a marked change in her. She became far more self indulgent—a more normal teenager—and took on a new confidence.

Every morning at 6.30 without fail, I would lie in bed planning exactly what I would and would not eat that day, and every night I would lie there and count up the calories of that meagre supply. In short, I was obsessed with food.

During the week I purged myself, starving myself, dreading the weekend ahead when I knew very well I was likely to go on a binge, eating all in sight, shovelling it in, to make up for what I had deprived myself of in the week. The guilt that followed these binges was unbearable. It made me lose any confidence I might have had in myself, and in my strict self-discipline which seemed all important, since it was what my brother lacked. My brother, older than I, was the black sheep of the family, who continually threatened the peace at home and who I think was the reason for my discipline neurosis.

Concentration became impossible. Even after a day of commuting to drama school where I exercised and danced for five hours, I could not or would not sit down and relax in front of the television. I wanted the family to be together but when we were I became irritable and nervous.

The preoccupation with food caused me to be extremely interested in cooking. I spent hours in the kitchen concocting dishes worthy of a cordon bleu certificate. Needless to say I took great pleasure in watching others eat my rich calorie-packed puddings and exotic gateaux, but not a morsel passed my lips.

Friends were amazingly patient. Knowing I would most probably refuse, they still invited me out. Baby sitting became a convenient excuse to avoid social events which threatened to include food and drink. My greatest enemy was the scales which I hopped on and off, on the sly, at least twice a day. My periods had been non-existent for a good two years; my hair was falling out; I had constant indigestion; looked like a bag of bones, and desperately needed help.

After fourteen weeks hospitalization on a strict regime, bed rest and family therapy I am now 28 lbs heavier, happy most of the time, and most important of all I understand myself far better than I ever have done. I can't say I know myself perfectly yet, but being able to answer for my actions and emotions is a much more positive way of going through life than denying my mind and my body.

I feel the time is ripe to leave home soon and begin to fend for myself, to prove myself. Brief, raucous rows are commonplace between the family—scenes I used to shun and fear, but I have learnt to express my true feelings, rather than ignoring and suppressing them.

I am not exactly sure what influenced these changes. Family therapy sessions, though they gave no solutions, helped me to understand myself, my family and other people.

I admit I have an occasional relapse; a binge maybe when I feel unhappy or bad about something, depressed, low, just as all healthy people feel now and again, but I don't have those old erroneous guilt pangs like I used to.

It was strangely exciting when I had my first period in four years, ten months after reaching my target weight. It was just like becoming a woman again—at the age of nineteen.

Having a boyfriend boosts anyone's ego, but when you have not been attracted to, or attractive to someone for several years, it certainly makes a difference. At last, as well as others valuing my own worth, I do too. I intend to respect both my body and my mind from now on.

Looking back over the last 7½ years to the time when our son was 13 years old and visibly starting anorexia nervosa, and knowing that even now, at 20 years old, it is still necessary for him to visit his London doctor on occasions, one realizes the seriousness of the condition and how difficult it is to completely "throw it off", even after many many months of treatment. But also to know that having gone through anorexia nervosa he is now leading a normal life, training for, hopefully, a future in agriculture on completing a three-year course this year, including a practical year involving hard physical work, lambing sheep, etc. one realizes that what looked an impossible dream some six years ago, is possible.

Our son arrived home from boarding school looking drawn and ill and continued to lose weight whilst at home; our biggest worry, at that time, was not knowing why. It was seven months before anorexia nervosa was diagnosed. Seven months of seeing our only son starving himself, being hospitalized in the local General to be encouraged to eat, but still unable to pinpoint the illness. The relief of being told "it's not cancer, it's not this, not that", but what is it? The coming home from hospital, and back to school as a day boy, we didn't dare let him board. The terrible frustration for his mother preparing all his favourite food and finding he would still eat only the absolute minimum.

Then a talk at a school function with a school Governor, he advised us to mention the name anorexia nervosa to his consultant, I wrote it down. This was the beginning of reaching the correct place to deal, we hoped, with the situation. The physician explained, anorexia = not eating, nervosa = nerves. Now at last our appointment with the psychiatrist and the day we shall never forget, our son was interviewed first, he came out with tears in his eyes—he'd been told. Our turn next, we came out wondering who was the patient, him or us.

Then to be told it is anorexia nervosa, a 50/50 chance of complete recovery and go into hospital for four months, we felt completely stunned. It is important to keep up the family contact while in hospital and driving 150 miles three times a week, we were grateful for the help and cooperation of family and friends in keeping up these visits. Our daughter, two years younger than her brother, of course had to be left more than one would like—instead of coming home from school to mum, it meant going to grandparents or friends. She obviously felt left out but didn't show it, and occasionally accompanied us to visit her brother at weekends.

Slowly seeing the weight return to our son, realizing what a long time it would take, but also realizing, at last, if a cure was possible this is where it would be done.

Eventually to have our son home again, looking so well, but alas after a while to see that weight disappearing again. The decision was eventually made, back into hospital. The strain during this period was not quite so great as our son was that much older, therefore it was not necessary to visit quite as often, but of course this time, although he was gaining weight, always with us was the thought "will he retain it?" Since this stay in hospital for another four months and by continuing to visit the doctor under whose care he is, he has improved physically and mentally to the situation of today.

What caused anorexia nervosa in our son? We do not know for certain and of course never will. Our only thoughts on the cause is that he developed physically very quickly and quite young, maybe mentally he could not cope. We often wonder, did something say, "if I stop eating, will I slow down and my friends catch up?"

My experience of anorexia goes back to 1970. My present age is 20 years old; height 5 feet 10 inches; weight 131 lbs.

The symptoms of anorexia started in 1970/71 in my second year at the boarding school I was sent to. I was then 13 years of age and weighed 135 lbs; height 5 feet 8 inches. I was extremely healthy and strong for my age. What happened was that I cut my diet right down, quite dramatically. Being at a boarding school and fed through a canteen system it was easy for me to skip meals, without staff realizing I was doing this, as normally they cannot stop boys from eating!

The other problem I had was convincing my fellow school friends who I lived with. The problem solved itself as they never took much notice, they just accepted I was a small eater, in fact after I had received treatment later on, I told them I had a physical condition, hence I could not eat a large quantity.

Whilst starving myself, I was going through agony, i.e. my stomach was shrinking and causing pain, also blood pressure went very low, and I passed out when standing up. Heavy nose bleeds were also a feature, but the main problem was trying to keep warm due to loss of weight. I found starving myself a great challenge, as I always loved food and eating, so stopping myself from doing this took a great deal of willpower.

By Christmas 1971 I was down to 98 lbs, of course my parents noticed I was looking ill and sent me to a medical consultant. He admitted me into an infirmary and did, I think, every medical test on me in the business, of course all proved negative.

Going back to why I stopped eating, I never have pinpointed why I did it. From what I remember, I felt I was getting overweight which connected with my worry of sexual attraction. After talking with the psychiatrist it was a type of rebellion against my parents for sending me to boarding school, which I hated. As far as relationships went, with my parents I never have thought it was too bad. Obviously now it is much better as I went through teenage strops against them. I always thought my father was a large (fat) man and I was determined never to be like him, also I found his temper affected me. As far as others were concerned, schoolboy relationships and later normal male to male relationships (not sexual) I did find difficult at times. As far as women were concerned, I took no interest as my preoccupation with food was the dominant thing in my life, in fact it took up most of my time.

It was not until I saw the psychiatrist that I realized I was ill. I was about 84 lbs at this stage and eating just two pieces of bread per day. I was amazed when the psychiatrist could tell me exactly how I thought and my devious means of getting out of eating. Thus I was admitted to hospital in 1971. I stayed for 4 months, left and lost all my weight again within a year. The reason I think was that I had no intention of keeping the weight on, I was so scared when in the unit I just conformed with the regime, but my attitude was not changed. Also going back to the same environment in boarding school did not help.

Thus in 1973 I was readmitted—but it was stipulated to me by the psychiatrist he could not readmit me again after this. The difference this time was, firstly that statement worried me, knowing survival might be difficult. I also stipulated that I stayed longer when at target weight (126 lbs) so as to adjust myself at this weight under supervision. The unit also proved to me that my perception of my body was wrong, i.e. I saw myself larger than I was! Also this time I was determined to stay at my target weight, but I was also determined not to kick the disease as I was worried of letting myself become obese. I left hospital at 129 lbs with this attitude of mind, hence a lot of my thoughts were preoccupied with controlled eating.

Today, six years later I weigh exactly the same as when I left hospital. Since then I have completed "O" levels and had two jobs as a farm worker, living on my own. This was difficult, but my determination to complete these jobs as a normal person was great, as the job was physically demanding. I am now in the final year of agricultural college, have a very understanding girlfriend who I can talk with and discuss my problems, which helps a great deal. In general I find it much easier to relate to people. My views on food are still that I am scared of kicking the disease but the preoccupation with food has reduced. In fact I eat and live a very normal life, except I keep a close watch on my weight and automatically respond. I still see the psychiatrist every six months.

To sum the whole thing up, I personally think that my determination not to eat was so great that if I had not had treatment I would not be here today.

An anorexic in the family was extremely disruptive of family life. C was totally concerned with herself and made demands for help and attention without regard for the comfort or desires of anyone else. At the start she was about 13 years old, and her brothers, aged 15 and 10 at that time, coped with the situation by ignoring it so far as possible. They were, of course, affected by the strain on the parents, and the time consumed with C meant less time was available for them. Happily this seems to have had no lasting effect, and now that C has recovered, her relationship with her brothers is amicable.

The greatest impact of C's anorexia was upon us, the parents. It was some time before we realized that anything was wrong. Then we discovered that C was starving herself in the midst of plenty, and this was almost beyond belief. We had never heard of anorexia nervosa and at this stage we tried to encourage or to bully her to eat, and this caused many quarrels and upheavals. Worry about her was constant, and the disturbed days and nights coping with tantrums and sobbing fits were many. Probably worse than this, and more difficult to come to terms with, was the antagonism, even hatred, that C often felt and expressed towards us. She sometimes made positive attempts to inflict mental pain and additional worry on us. Except that we (the parents) became convinced that C needed professional help, we did not agree on the way to handle her, the father favouring a "softer" approach than the mother. This disagreement placed further strains on our marriage, which was already suffering from the effects of worry and taut nerves.

At first we reacted sharply against the suggestion that C might have to enter hospital. Looking back now, it is difficult to find the reason for this reaction, but possibly it was connected with this sense of disbelief that anyone could do this to themselves.

C returned from holiday so emaciated that there was no alternative to her entering a hospital. She went to a general hospital where they saved her life by feeding her. We found, both then and later, that C submitted to a high calorie diet in hospital with little fuss, apparently resigning herself once the decisions about eating were taken from her. She received no psychiatric help, and upon discharge she soon started to lose weight again. She now had another rod to beat us with, in her bad times we had made her go to hospital.

The turning point in the illness came when she was admitted to the next hospital, and received the specific course of treatment for anorexia nervosa. I must utter a word of warning. Just as the illness grew so slowly, and at times seemed to be improving, so the recovery was slow, and at times she relapsed. I cannot emphasize too strongly the immense importance we attach to the very long period, two to three years, that C spent as an outpatient. C desperately needed someone she could trust outside her family, with whom to discuss her problems. Although at times C fought against us, for most of the time she desperately wanted to get better, and underwent the treatment voluntarily.

What caused it? We do not know. C was a normal happy schoolgirl, and there were no exceptional tensions or upsets in the home—nothing that we have been able to recall at all events. In the early days of her anorexia, C expressed fears of sex; of the decisions that she would have to make as an adult; and of dying. She had received sex instruction well before the illness, and so far as this family is concerned, this was just one of all manner of subjects that the children could, and did, discuss with us if they desired.

C has now recovered and is living a normal life with its usual ups and downs. Living with an anorexic is living on a knife edge where the slightest word or action can send you into a world of sobbing and screaming and wild accusations. It takes time to get over this, to stop being apprehensive of disaster when your daughter bursts into tears.

We have got there at last.

I am very glad to say that I am finding it increasingly difficult to remember the details of my emotions and life at the time of this horrifying illness. This means that more and more I can live my life to the full without its shadow hanging over me.

I contracted anorexia at about the age of 12½ although it progressed very gradually and I did not believe that there was anything wrong with me. It was my parents who dragged me to the doctors, worried out of their minds. All I remember of that time is that my sole concern was food and what I was not going to eat. My school work did not suffer at first, quite the opposite, as all my energy went into it. I suppose my first realization that there was something wrong with me was when I found it so hard to chat to the other girls at school. I just used to be there, staring at nothing. A friend once told me that I used to be quite popular, as I was always fairly lively and friendly, but now they did not know how to treat me. They could not be themselves with me any more because I had changed so much. I was getting worse and the gap between me and my world and other people was getting wider.

The most frightening thing I have found since getting better is when I meet an anorexic and see and hear what I used to be like. An anorexic is completely shut off from the world that most people know. They rarely notice interactions between other people, food and weight are the most important things. We used to have terrible rows at home because I wouldn't eat any dinner, or if mum and dad persuaded me to, I used to get so hysterical and upset that in the end I had used up all the food I had eaten in nervous energy. Energy is the other obsession of the anorexic. Whether I had eaten or not I used to exercise to "burn it off", running everywhere, always trying to do something active. Whatever weight I was, be it 80 or 90 lbs I had to lose "just a little bit more".

By now my school work was failing because I had to devote all my time to the avoidance of eating food, weighing myself, and exercising. I would dispose of my lunch, then if I weighed myself as soon as I got home I should have lost another couple of pounds, and if I didn't have any dinner and then weighed myself again I might have lost some more!

I used to cook a great many cakes and biscuits. I never ate them I just used to make them so that I could smell them and look at them and watch other people eat them, but not me! I used to go out, but only because I wanted to use up energy not because I wanted my friends' company, and when I was out I just wanted to go home again. I didn't want to have to think or make decisions, I just wanted to be looked after.

By now my mother was looking ill herself because she didn't know what to do with me. My father seemed to understand a little more, and used to spend hours talking to me and I was so horrible to both of them.

My first stay in hospital was in a general hospital. There, I was put on bed rest and stuffed with as much food as they could get down me. The psychiatrist I was under never came to see me while I was in the hospital and I used to get terribly upset. It was during this time that my father realized that it was psychiatric help I needed.

Our doctor told us about more specialized psychiatric help and we sought it. After two–three years of this illness, I myself felt I wanted to get better and it was I who made the decision to go in for treatment. This is very important as the girl herself must want to get better for anything to work.

The new psychiatric treatment runs parallel with a high calorie diet. They do not allow your weight to go up in leaps and bounds as they do in general hospitals. Weight and food intake are very carefully controlled, and once the target weight has been reached the girls are allowed up for increasing periods of time. The stay after weight-reaching is very important because the staff help the girls to come to terms with their weight and the difference they feel at being a normal weight.

I was lucky, my parents were never ashamed that their daughter was in a psychiatric unit, as there was no need to be. However, I know that some girls' parents were horrified at their daughter being in such a place. This didn't help the girls as they had made the difficult decision to get better and then faced opposition from their parents. I believe that the treatment I received is about the best treatment an anorexic can receive if she is ever to lead a full life again. Even after leaving hospital it is a gradual process of learning to live in the outside world. Weight and food no longer control my life, and I enjoy going out and being with friends, going dancing, studying and all the things that enrich life. I do still get depressed but not to the extent that I used to and not for such long periods of time.

To any anorexic who is just existing in that horrible world I would say to take the plunge and undergo treatment. The thought is horrifying at the moment but believe me with help the weight will not be so terrible and your whole outlook on life will change and you will be able to live again.

In retrospect, at its chronic stage, anorexia was more than a condition affecting me, it was the fundamental factor affecting every aspect of my life; it was my identity.

I cannot explain exactly why it should have afflicted me. Now, after much probing and questioning I think that it was the cumulative result of stress at home and school, reacting against a self-image which had it roots in childhood feelings and experiences.

As long as I can remember, I had needed to please my parents, whilst knowing that their compliant, successful daughter was really an egocentric monster, capable of who knows what atrocities. I yearned to please them and cared desperately for their approval.

During my teens I was aware of the indistinct but certain knowledge that my father strongly disapproved of disco's, parties and boyfriends; the usual paraphernalia of adolescence. Unconsciously therefore I shied away from these things. I buried myself in an ever-growing mound of schoolwork, glad of an excuse to avoid an aspect of my life which scared me. I allowed links with school-friends to lapse and became withdrawn and depressed.

This decline accelerated rapidly one school holiday while my father was in hospital. My mother was swamped by the demands of home and office, and I was left alone and I soon enmeshed myself in a cast iron discipline of schoolwork and dieting.

I lost weight rapidly and became very depressed, although convinced that as soon as I wanted I could stop dieting. I refused to do this though, as I felt that dieting was the key to the success I was achieving in my school work. After abortive visits to a G.P. I was referred to a psychiatrist specializing in "this kind of thing".

I was admitted immediately to an anorexic unit. This was the first time I had been definitely associated with the term and it seemed a case of ludicrously mistaken diagnosis, although not entirely unsatisfactory; to me it implied an illness that kept girls slim.

The reality of the treatment was far less appealing. I was incarcerated in a small room with five other anorexics. Treatment was oriented entirely around food and weight. Washing, dressing, visitors and mobility all depended on consuming vast quantities of unappetizing food and gaining weight as quickly as possible. Through my fellow patients, many of whom were chronic long-term sufferers I quickly absorbed every possible subtlety of anorexic behaviour.

On discharge I felt committed to losing weight. I think now I wanted to prove I still held the reins of control over my body, and also that I still had a problem to be sorted out. Inevitably I was readmitted, and this pattern continued for two years. I was four times in that hospital, and once underwent a serious stomach operation; the result of overfeeding a hideously abused stomach.

Curiously, the certain knowledge of the treatment awaiting me never acted as a deterrent. On discharge the realities of treatment became hazy. Hospital to me meant somewhere free of the anxiety of schoolwork, where people were interested in me and where the rigid discipline absolved me of needing to make decisions I was scared and unable to make. Although depserately unhappy I could not imagine a life free of a see-saw weight gain and loss and hospitalization.

I was transferred to another specialist. His treatment consisted of a slow weight increase whilst examining minutely with me and my parents my life, feelings, and personal relationships. I learnt much but still could not face a life any different from the pattern of the last few years.

On discharge however, instead of starting my studies once more, I took a job. An imperceptible change occurred in my attitude. I saw that "normal" people around me, free of the obsessions of weight and avoiding food were happy, certainly happier than me. I began to resent this self-hung millstone. At this time I contacted a self-help group run for sufferers, past and present. They showed me that anorexia was not a life sentence: anorectics could be happy and "normal".

I approached and overcame the hurdle of gaining weight. I was then faced with reabsorbing myself into a society I had alienated myself from. I put my confidence in the group and faced the guilt, anxiety and terror of a "normal" life.

Having resolved the initial problem of weight gain others remain. I am still undergoing a compressed adolescence, and am trying to cope with the responsibilities of a job, sharing a flat and trying to handle relationships.

Mentally, a pre-occupation with food and weight lingers, but I feel this is under control. I am now trying to discover who and what I am, and am determined to like and accept whatever emerges.

Professional background. Mother eccentric, gifted, "beyond reproach". Acted as if husband was a tyrant but she was actually dominant. Father ordinary, explosive temper. No effective say in management of children. Very unhappy marriage, violent rows. Mother increasingly depressed. One older brother considered fun but "bad". A cold ignorant nannie.

Rigid upbringing to age 2½ when my will had been deliberately broken by mother, she told me this when I was older. Loved and overadmired but physical show of affection was mocked at from birth. Father afraid to show his very real affection. Particularly shielded from adult world. Childhood attempts at friendships and all adults were criticised, especially father. All males were bad. Was painfully self conscious. Secretly analytical, critical and determined. In certain areas obsessive and perfectionist. Quite unable to be naughty. Strong compassion for (identification with) those I thought unjustly treated, especially mother. Seldom admitted distress. Early fears for mother's safety. After age eight strong masochistic fantasies with sexual arousal.

Sexual taboos strong. Thoughts of marriage disgusting. Breast must be disguised. Very strongly guarded against masturbation. Told childbirth was lonely and excruciating. Did not understand sex until age 18.

Kind but inhibited governess to age 10.

At school—the late start, social gaucheness, over-anxiety to please and a feeling of being an outsider because difference in religion forbade sharing in common worship, all combined to cause secret loneliness, compensated by hard work, over-achievement all along.

Happier in small friendly groups—Girl Guides, Sunday School. Bond with mother increased by much fun together over studies, general discussions, and outdoor activities.

No nice clothes—school uniform only. Occasionally dressed "as mother's doll", she used to say this.

Periods started age 10½. No shock, but embarrassing. Comfort in eating encouraged. Very unhappy at resulting weight gain—147 lbs from 14 yrs, and breast size.

All these factors led to my being subconsciously terrified of growing up into the adult sexual world, especially when I had to leave my mother's companionship and protection.

Age 16½ father left home. Immediate onset of Raynaud's syndrome (cold extremities). Mother incapacitated by depression. Boarding school and separation from home for eight months—immediately periods ceased, followed by loss of 60 lbs in weight.

I had intention of slimming. Innate masochism and determination enabled me to avoid food. Purging. Grossly overactive despite extreme exhaustion. Hair fell out. Skin got dry. Sexual fantasies ceased. Thought belt was stretching and mirrors distorting. Obsessional thinking about food.

Age 17½ returned to mother who, shocked, suggested a nursing home but, needing her, I wept hysterically. Persuaded a doctor to prescribe thyroid for my cold extremities!

Protected from "life fears" with mother I ate better, often secretly. Stopped purging. Still overactive. No longer exhausted. Frequent "homing" to mother over the years prevented further weight loss. Loose clothes disguised thinness.

Almost from the start I knew what I was doing to myself, though not the subconscious mechanism. I believe my mother colluded with me from now on.

As marriage was "out" I was ambitious for a career—wanted to tell mothers how to feed their families! Fear of naked body precluded nursing. Decided to take a science degree and enter a caring profession.

At college—same pattern. Studied excessively except at one period when health and spirits failed. Inability to eat with others prevented companionship. I seemed to want "not to show". Developed painful vitamin and circulatory deficiencies.

After about three years, kind companions led me to gradual socialization, especially after boost to morale on graduation. Overactivity ceased. Longer happier periods from home. However sharing of meals now led to a vicious circle of induced vomiting, which caused cramps, irresistible hunger, stealing food and gorging with tremendous guilt. Weight rose to 105 lbs.

Until now my mother had destroyed friendships, now she began to enjoy hints of romances. A young barrister fell in love with me, or rather with my sexual "purity". Overwhelmed with oceanic feelings of gratitude and unworthiness, I wanted to run away, but with the fascination of his love and my mother's manipulation of us (she had now become emotionally involved with him) moderate petting occurred. With the resulting flood of sexual desire circulation improved and appetite, weight, and periods became, and remained, completely normal after 10 years illness. Weight 120 lbs.

When my mother said we must marry I jumped at it—released—with false compassion and normal desires. I gradually realized that the marriage would be disastrous—black depression lay ahead. But my extreme masochism and the dominance now of my fiancé instead of my mother, who had now turned aggressively against him, led me on in defiance of her and my better judgement.

We had several children. Sex life was unsatisfactory. After years of overwork, extraordinary masochistic servility, depression and confusion, chaos threatened us all.

At this point I obtained the help I had always sensed I needed. I gradually saw where false projections and abnormal interdependence lay, cutting me off from my inner confident "female" self and so had half paralysed me.

Things began to improve, not entirely—partners thus chosen have complimentary problems—but life became possible for us all and I eventually found an inner peace.

I think that sufferers from anorexia nervosa need firm encouragement to face their condition honestly and to seek help actively, with ongoing support—especially for their feminine self esteem. Also that underlying complexes need disentangling so that their full nature can be integrated and lives fulfilled.

I think that the change in our daughter's mental and physical condition was something that occurred gradually so that at first I did not take it too seriously. Here, I thought was a teenager's attempt to be "in the fashion" with a nice slim model girl figure. Slim, figure hugging trousers and jeans were very popular. However, this slimming seemed to get out of control. From being a well built, happy, athletic teenage schoolgirl she soon became a white faced, irritable, walking skeleton. The more we tried to get her to eat, the more she rebelled. At the same time, she seemed to get a kind of satisfaction in cooking huge meals for the rest of us. She was interested in cooking, and when at home, would spend a lot of time in the kitchen, where she would keep "picking" at the various dishes, but always declining a proper meal herself. Her diet seemed to consist of black coffee and small salads. We didn't really know what to do. We had never heard of anorexia nervosa until a friend showed us an article about it in a magazine. Later on we saw a programme on TV about it, and then we began to understand a little of what was happening. I think that if we had known about anorexia nervosa earlier we might have coped better with the situation.

Our daughter's troubles seemed to start around the time she left school. In her early teens she was a happy energetic girl, played plenty of sport, athletics, swimming, and hockey, and was Head Girl of her House at School. She seemed quite confident in most things, tended to be a leader in some ways. She would organize some of our neighbours' children, one or two who were a bit backward, into a little class and give them lessons. She took learning to drive a car in her stride, passing her test at the first attempt. However she was always nervous at examination times, and the top of her bed clothes would be dotted with teeth marks. She was very disappointed in only getting one "A" level result, and this was when her condition seemed to change. She also seemed to be unsure of herself in relationships with boy-friends. Her choice of boy-friends was perhaps not the best, and never seemed to develop on a permanent basis. One of her boy-friends was a physical education teacher, and possibly an innocent remark of his may have decided her to lose weight. She tended to be immature in some ways. A lot of her letters to us after she left home to go to a hospital to train were a bit childlike, with funny little sketches, caricatures and arrows etc. dotted about.

We would get numerous frantic telephone calls, which seemed to be a cry for help but we didn't seem to be able to get through to her. All the time her mental and physical condition seemed to get worse. She abandoned practically all her school friends, and when she came home on weekend visits would never go out socially, saying she had nowhere to go and no one to meet. Sometimes we would persuade her to come out to a restaurant for a meal. She would enjoy it at the time, but afterwards would be angry and miserable because she had eaten it. She was literally a bag of bones.

It was a great relief to us when finally she consented to have medical treatment for her condition. I could never quite understand, when she was working in a hospital, in daily contact with doctors, nurses, consultants etc. how long it took for something to be done. Possibly the first step had to come from our daughter herself. It was a very worrying time for us, especially for my wife, who always seemed to be on the receiving end of the frustrating telephone calls. Many of these calls were at the time of her final exams. She was very worried that she would not pass.

At this time, I think she was well aware of her problem but seemed unable to solve it on her own initiative. The hospital treatment came not a moment too soon, and the staff at the hospital deserve much credit for getting her and the other girls back to a more normal state of mind.

She is obviously much better now, but I think that her condition is more being "held under control" rather than being completely cured. One problem is I think, her continuing stomach pains. Perhaps if she could get rid of those, she would be more inclined to eat normally and regularly. The other problem is, I think, that she still seems unable to strike up a genuine long-lasting relationship with the opposite sex, and I think this causes her some concern.

I do not know how I got anorexia or what started it off. Girls of my age are very conscious of their weight and size, and are endlessly going on diets in the hope of slimming. Being in a girls' school, therefore, surrounded by plump girls trying to lose a few pounds may very likely have influenced me, and started me slimming too.

I have always been thin, so it is puzzling that I should want to diet, but I decided that I would like to be just a little bit thinner than I was. So I started to cut down on food. My parents were amused, and not in the least worried, for at this stage I was only cutting down on one or two pieces of toast and cake at tea. They did not think it would last. However, I went on dieting and began to cut down on more and more foods. It became an obsession and gradually led to anorexia.

At first, cutting down on certain foods and eating less had no effect on me, but as it became more serious, and cutting down increased, I began to experience some of the worst conditions of the illness. I would get tired very easily and quickly, and I started to lose my energy. With the weakness, tiredness and lack of energy came depressions. Before I became anorexic I was quite cheerful, but I started to feel moody and depressed. I got upset and depressed at the smallest thing. If someone whistled whilst at table, I became so irritated that I just shouted at them. I also began to get obsessed with food and meals. I did not mind preparing meals and watching people eat them. I would spend all morning thinking about lunch, which I then began to prepare about an hour before that was necessary. I am still very conscious of food and I go on making meals and plying food on others. I would also be able to give an exact description later of someone's meal and the quantities they ate, if I had been sitting at their table.

I am very aware of my size, and do all I can to look as thin as possible. When I was at my worst, I used to wear a blue denim skirt as often as I could because I had been told that I looked particularly thin and dreadful in it. I still try to look thinner than I am, especially while I am at school. As I walk about the school, I breathe in; I wear as few clothes as possible, because I feel that an extra layer of clothing will make me look much fatter. Out of doors I only wear an unbuttoned coat, and never any gloves or scarves. As a result, I am nearly always cold, even indoors. My hands go a sort of purple colour and become so numb that I can hardly write. However, although I know that they are dreadful-looking, I like it when people comment on them, because I feel that it shows I have anorexia. I feel proud of them, and until I am by myself or at home, I make no attempt to warm them up.

I wear my watchstrap very loose on my wrist so that it can slide up and down on my arm, because I think that my wrist then looks thinner. I feel that walking about silently shows that you are less heavy. Therefore I creep about the house, and up and down stairs, so that nobody hears me coming, and I often give people great frights when I walk into rooms.

One of my greatest fears is that other girls in my class will get anorexia too. I want to be the only girl in the class, even in the school, to have the illness. Whenever I think that someone might have it, I watch them closely and ask them roundabout questions about food and what they eat, until I can satisfy myself that nobody else has it. However, now a girl in my class has got anorexia. I have been watching her closely, suspecting that she did, and I was very upset when I heard that she did. I was not upset for her sake, but upset because she had got the illness that I wanted to have for myself. I have got over the news a bit, but I am still rather depressed about it, and always hope that she does not look as thin as I do.

I do not think that I see myself or others to be their true size. I am always worrying about whether so-and-so is thinner than I, although to other people it is perfectly obvious that I am at least three times thinner. Whenever I look at myself in the mirror, I never think how thin I am, I always think the opposite: how fat I am.

I started having treatment when I was already past my worst. Although I was by no means recovered, I had begun to eat more and was gradually enjoying doing things again, such as buying clothes and going out with people. (Another aspect of my anorexia was that I became very unsociable, and refused invitations to go out with friends.) My energy was beginning to come back and so was confidence. Treatment has helped to increase this confidence and to sort out the numerous problems of the illness. Although I did discuss them with my parents, I felt a bit freer to discuss them with a doctor. However, whether or not I would have recovered without the aid of any treatment I simply cannot tell.

I became anorectic when I was about 17 although I think that the roots of the illness were there long before this. It has been fairly difficult to give a "potted" version, I would need a book to cover all the aspects contributing to my condition.

During this time in my life, my prime interest was my shape. I was constantly looking in mirrors or pinching myself to discover the depth of my fat. I just had to be moving all the time—I would walk everywhere or would fidget continuously if forced to sit. I became bored very quickly and always wanted to be moving onto something new.

I just knew that I was too fat although I rarely weighed myself. Even at my lowest weight (84 lbs) I refused to believe that I was too thin. I used to judge myself by my clothes—I could not bear anything tight as it might mean I had gained weight. I used to read anything concerned with slimming and knew the calorific value of most things. I used to love cooking exotic things and watching others eating them, not that I ever ate anything of them.

I was firmly convinced my diet was healthy. I thought I was getting all the vitamins and minerals I needed without any dreaded fats. I would eat vast piles of vegetables at my only daily meal. I ate very little protein, just an occasional egg. My hair began to fall out but I did not worry. I would feel guilty if I ate any more. I drank a lot of tea and water—I suppose to fill my stomach with something although I'd learnt to ignore my hunger pangs. I started smoking heavily, presumably as an appetite suppressant. My bowels became an obsession with me. I would feel my abdomen was too large if I had not been. I dreaded eating with others as then I could not avoid eating more than I wanted. I became cunning and devised means of disguising how little I had eaten. I would go out in the kitchen for second helpings (of vegetables) and dispose carefully of the meat previously hidden by some vegetables. I found that I just had to make myself vomit after meals if I thought I had eaten too much. I felt disgusted with myself at first but these feelings became less eventually.

Anorexia represented a means of coping with my gross lack of self confidence. I had always been plump as a child—taunts of being Bessie Bunter used to hurt. I felt too fat to participate in any games and thus felt alienated at times. This almost self-induced alienation became particularly bad during my adolescent years. I could not cope with that and trying to establish a life for myself outside of home and school. I began to feel very inadequate and thought that nobody would find me interesting enough to want to know. I lost some weight through conscious dieting and immediately felt more attractive. I was determined that I wouldn't put on any more weight—my new slim figure represented my means of having a large circle of friends and interesting life style.

I was having problems at home. My parents were worried that my new found social life would endanger my studies. I had always been good at school—I'd regarded it as my saving grace when I was a child and it meant a lot to me. They put subtle pressure on me. I couldn't cope with their plans for me and my own being so different. I found escape in losing more weight—almost as if I wanted to physically escape the situation. This was complicated by the fact that my boyfriend and I had begun to have sex together. Although I wanted this and wanted my boyfriend and I to stay together, I couldn't cope with my parents' obvious fears for me. It was so much easier to avoid the confrontation. I desperately did not want to be any trouble, although ironically, it would have eventually been much easier if I had asserted myself more. My weight continued to fall, I began to study harder than ever and I began to lose all interest in sex. My periods stopped but I was not worried at all.

It was only on moving away from home, in the course of my job, that I realized how distorted my views had become. I met a new circle of friends who I felt liked me for the person I really was. I was away from parental pressure and was no longer overpowered by them. I had some dealings with anorexia at work and had to face the fact that I was anorectic. I was still afraid however that if my anorexia was taken away, there would be little left to my personality. It represented a whole life style to me and I felt that my trendy, thin shape gave me something to be proud of.

Treatment was difficult. I found it very difficult to realize that I was not as worthless as I believed. It was difficult to believe that my new found confidence would not disappear when I gained weight. It's been very much an ongoing thing. I feel my personality has been developing all the time since my discharge from hospital, almost as if it had been repressed while anorexic.

I still cannot tolerate any weight gain of over a few pounds. My diet is still fairly rigid, finely balanced so that I do not gain any weight. I allow myself an occasional lapse but not by too much or else I feel guilty.

I realize I have my own life to live and that I cannot consider others to the exclusion of my own wishes. I have since married and I find sex enjoyable. I am not frightened now of my own sexuality as it does not represent a threat now I am not worried about my parents' wishes. I feel that my new found confidence has a real basis now and can only regret the three or four years I wasted as I was too afraid to fight for my own wishes.

I understand that the medical definition for anorexia nervosa is loss of appetite together with nervous and hysterical symptoms. This, as regards myself is not quite so—I have always had, and I think always will have, a roaring appetite. Another definition of the disease is a compulsive slimming complaint, which I think is more applicable, though there must be a deep, deep rooted reason behind all this, which I do not know.

I was a bonny baby, and remained chubby throughout my childhood and teenage years. At the age of 18 I weighed 163 lbs with a bust measurement of 38 ins. Being fat did not worry me and I had plenty of boyfriends. Then I became pregnant and married against my parents' wishes. It was after the birth of my child that my nervous trouble started. With moderate dieting I went down to 126 lbs, and was really pleased with my new figure and felt quite fit. Suddenly, when my child was about a year old, I found that I could not go out without experiencing the most horrifying panic attacks. I realized that I was suffering from agoraphobia—my mother, being an agoraphobic, was extremely sympathetic, and I went to the family doctor, who prescribed some drugs. My mother was so understanding and helpful, I now realize how ghastly she must have felt when, as a child, I recall she would not go out. I found the doctor's tablets pretty useless, and one day after lunch I swallowed them all. I panicked, realizing that I did not want to die, and was taken into hospital urgently . . . later, after three months at home with my parents it was decided that I should return to my own home and my husband. My marriage had not been happy, and I had become frigid. We agreed on sleeping separately, but after two weeks all the symptoms returned, so I ran back to my mother. I then found myself a boyfriend and my husband divorced me.

Now back to my earlier weight and having been deserted by my boyfriend, I developed into a compulsive eater, and on reaching 142 lbs, I consulted my doctor who gave me some slimming tablets. I lost weight and was once again 126 lbs. Unfortunately once off the tablets, I started gobbling everything in sight. For several years I was on one form of appetite suppressing drug or another whilst my weight swung wildly between 126 and 140 lbs.

Next, I became pregnant again and had the baby adopted. I now weighed 168 lbs and dieted. I reached 115 lbs and felt marvellous.

As had been predicted, I became pregnant for the third time. I married the father, following his divorce. After the birth I weighed 166 lbs and dieted down to 112 lbs without the aid of drugs. My marriage was not happy—I had once again become frigid. Quite suddenly I stopped eating. I went to my separate bed at 8.0 p.m. and woke at 3.0 a.m. I couldn't stop working. I was obsessed with cleaning cupboards, washing and polishing floors. I had an abundance of energy. I was 94 lbs. I was offered admission to hospital and after refusing, was warned that I might have to be admitted on an involuntary basis. This I regarded as ridiculous—I felt physically fit—and, on being told that I could possibly drop dead at any time, I almost laughed. I ceased to menstruate. I refused to accept the fact that I was ill. Then I started bingeing again and decided after all to enter hospital. I underwent hypnosis. This had a miraculous effect—I ate with relish and without feelings of guilt and depression. This feeling lasted for one day, and the following day I ate and drank because I was compelled to, not because I wanted or felt the need to. I often ate like a horse, and my weight shot up to 105 lbs. Then again I would manage to eat nothing for days on end. My weight yo-yoed between 92 lbs and 100 lbs. Next I became thoroughly bored and rather depressed and spent a whole week eating my way through pounds of goodies provided at the hospital. My weight shot up to 108 lbs and in a blind panic I discharged myself against advice, and returned home to my husband.

Within a couple of weeks my weight had gone down to 92 lbs and I was bouncing about full of the same nervous energy and sleeping separately from my husband. Suddenly I developed a compulsive urge to eat and became increasingly frustrated. I then had the idea of taking laxatives, in the hope that what I had eaten might "whoosh" through me. I bought my first packet of chocolate Ex-Lax.

I struggled on fighting my appetite. I then found that I could not bear to be alone at home. My appetite became uncontrollable. I downed a full bottle of Tofranil and Valium, and came round once again in a hospital bed.

It was the same old pattern. One day compulsive eating and then starvation for as long as I could bear. I still struggled with the Ex-Lax which my family brought in at my request. I found that two pieces at night produced a rush of water the following morning, and my weight was the same as it had been before my "nosh-up". I decided to have a good feast every Friday. It delighted my mother to see me tucking into my food, when I visited her on that day each week. I managed to get away with my early morning diarrhoea on Saturdays and no one was aware of what was going on. My weight dropped from 98 lbs down to 90 lbs and I was delighted. Now nothing could persuade me to go back to hospital. I was mentally the same as before, always turning out cupboards and dashing about in a frenzy, going to bed exhausted at 7.30 p.m. and rising at 3.0 a.m.

The Ex-Lax became less and less effective, until I was convinced that I had ruined my bowel. I became lethargic, and panic-stricken at the thought of going out alone. This I put down to undernourishment, and too much Ex-Lax. I found great difficulty in getting to sleep, even under sedation. I also found that if I ate after taking my nightly tablets, I would go out like a light, so I saved my daily meal until bedtime. If I ate during the day, I would rush straight onto the bathroom scales, and that would be that—more Ex-Lax if need be.

Although I made a great effort and ate practically every evening, I started to experience various disturbing symptoms. Instead of regaining my former energy, I became more and more lethargic, my heart banged furiously and although I was hungry, my mouth became so dry that I could hardly get any food down.

Even my daily treat of a bar of chocolate would stick at the back of my throat. I developed an obsession about weighing myself. I was on the bathroom scales at least 20 times a day. I became very dizzy and tense, and could not understand what was wrong. I realize now that subconsciously I did not want to eat, or rather put on weight, and I was suffering from fear that I might. My weight was 81 lbs.

During this time, my husband had fallen for a teenage girl and wanted a divorce, which I duly gave him. My weight now rose to 151 lbs. This depressed me a great deal. Once again I tried dieting and I really got going. My diet was a starvation diet. Gradually, my craving for sweet things decreased, until I was eating nothing but a handful of nuts and occasional hard boiled egg. My weight dropped to under 100 lbs. I was once again full of energy, up at 5.0 a.m. polishing furniture, taking and fetching my daughter from school.

Of course, having reached 98 lbs I wanted more weight off. I had anorexia again. By April I was 80 lbs and felt very fit. Then I started eating again, because I knew that it was dangerous for me to drop below 84 lbs. I consulted my doctor and he arranged for me to see a psychiatrist again. Panic stricken, I stuffed myself with food and five days later, when I saw the psychiatrist, I was 86 lbs. Much to my relief, I was not detained, but warned that if I lost more weight I would have to be admitted.

The other day after eating some nuts I had an attack of violent retching, without bringing anything up. I am now terrified of going out for fear that the same thing may happen again in public, or that I may have diarrhoea, and lose control. I force myself to take and fetch my child from school, but some days I simply cannot do it. Some days I am below 84 lbs, other days I am above. Today I am 87 lbs having retained two days' food. I have days when I feel so sick that I cannot eat, or else I start eating, develop a burning thirst, drink gallons of water or coffee, thus filling my stomach to the point, I feel, of perforation. All my energy has gone, I am very blown out, and feel rather depressed. I know that I am the only one who can help myself now. I can be taken into hospital, built up, only to come out and diet again.

I do not know how much longer I can keep up this struggle to put on some weight, when subconsciously I do not want to eat. All I know is that eating makes me depressed and lethargic. I do not know how to behave. Starvation for me is the height of satisfaction. One theory is that I do this to punish myself, for what I do not know. Another theory is that I have a subconscious desire to make myself sexually unattractive to men, but I am not aware of this, though I have no desire for intercourse, which is, I understand, another symptom of anorexia.

There is so much more that I could write . . .

Anorexia is such a bewildering illness, for the victim and possibly more so for those around her, that it's impossible to describe articulately and coherently the multifarious factors involved. I still, after all these years, have moments when I can hardly believe that I've spent half my life in the grip of a phobia which to many appears quite bizarre and incomprehensible.

Yet it's a very logical illness in some ways. What could be more rational for someone who can't cope with life, than to literally fade away from it? However varied the specific causes of anorexia may be, I don't think anyone would dispute the definition of the illness as a symptom of a fundamental inability to face physical, sexual and emotional maturity. I know this is true of myself; and in retrospect, it is not difficult to appreciate the mounting pressures which accumulated to such an unbearable extent during my teens that I developed anorexia as my refuge.

My memory of childhood is dominated by painful emotion, guilt, fear, a need to be "special", an obsession with my imaginary unpopularity, also insecurity, despite my loving and protective (over-protective?) family environment. Of these emotions, guilt was the most pernicious. I don't remember ever being without a searing conscience, pervading my whole body and mind; I used to pray to a God (in whom I had no belief) to protect me from blindness and death, both of which I was convinced were about to strike. I lived under a compulsion to make constant "confessions" to those around me, for any trivial crime I might commit and hard upon the relief of one confession would follow the necessity to create another crime demanding another confession. What I also remember clearly, although I don't know at what age it occurred, was a moment when the realization flooded over me that I had been guilty of such evil, for which there was no means of atonement, that my future could consist only of wretchedness and loneliness. I've never since been able to glimpse any potential source of goodness in my life without destroying it.

My emotions as a child and teenager were strong—whether or not they were more intense than "normal", I can't, of course, judge. From about the age of twelve I was very aware of the attraction I felt towards the opposite sex, and conscious of the strength of feeling involved—physical, sexual and emotional. I was also painfully mindful of my own unattractiveness, which in my view comprised far more than a tendency towards overweight, although that *was* a factor. I felt generally unwholesome. I had friendships with boys, but never a physical relationship, which was something I knew was denied to me. Probably my transference at the age of fifteen from a conventional girls' day school to a mixed boarding school exacerbated my feelings—certainly I suffered considerable inner torment, which I attempted to combat by retiring into a deliberate silent, uncommunicative, protective shell, though my eating was not at first affected.

The emphasis on the family as the most powerful influence on emotional development has obviously led me, over the years, to spend considerable thought on the subject—and there are disturbing elements. It becomes increasingly clear to me as I grow older and wiser, that my father (now dead) was an extremely unhappy man, suffering long periods of severe depression, and sadly inhibited emotionally. He was a loving and gentle father, but the two factors which remain firmly in my mind are his assertion that he didn't need anyone, and his frequent reference to his hatred of being "ordinary". I've never learnt the exact nature of my mother's problems, but the fact that she used to beat herself compulsively is sufficient evidence that those problems were formidable. I always felt the need to assure the outside world of the perfect nature of my parent's relationship—whereas I'm aware now that it must have been fraught with tension and strain. I suppose my environment was deceptive. I was surrounded by a united family who loved me, valued me highly, and wanted everything that was best for me; great care was taken to prepare me for the physical changes of puberty and adolescence, yet at the same time I sensed a disapproval of all the feelings that were stirring within me; and I'm convinced that I grew up in the midst of an emotional volcano which constantly smouldered but was never allowed to erupt. The atmosphere was thick with stifled emotion, the recollection of which still overpowers me every time I set foot in my parental home.

My attitude towards food during those early years is difficult to recall, it seems unbelievable now that there was ever a time when food was not an obsession, a time when I could eat normally and naturally. There was always plenty of appetizing food available at home, and I know I sometimes felt miserable on account of over-indulgence. In my teens I did become too heavy, and I was acutely sensitive to any remarks concerning my size or appetite. But I don't remember an excessive emphasis on food in our household—although there are a few memories which seem significant; before meals I used to go round the whole house checking that every door was shut, and only then could I sit down at the table. It wasn't unusual for my mother to go for several days eating virtually nothing, although we've discussed this in the light of my illness, I think she's probably being honest when she claims she genuinely didn't feel hungry, or simply couldn't be bothered. More significant I think is the fact that at home my father couldn't bring himself to eat everything on his plate; he always left something, as though full acceptance of what my mother had provided was more than he could bear, and he had to reject at least part of what she offered. When he ate in a restaurant he was able to clean his plate, and also eat certain items of food which he wouldn't touch at home. I think it's quite possible that as a sensitive child I might have unwittingly absorbed the concept of food as a potential emotional weapon.

At the time of the outbreak of my illness, when I was 17 my life was to all appearances full of promise, I was academically successful, and my talent for tennis was drawing considerable attention. Inwardly, it was a time of emotional chaos, constant anxiety, and relentless hammering from my overwhelming conscience. Then a powerful force inside me, stronger than anything I've ever known before or since, dictated that I must embark on a rigid course of self-starvation. It was something infinitely more complex than a conscious decision to lose weight. The initial result, apart from rapid weight loss, was a feeling of exhilaration verging on euphoria, because at that time, in my total unawareness of what was happening to me, starvation brought with it a conviction that I'd discovered a way of making life tolerable, and a means of expiating my guilt. I was intoxicated by a sense of power, a sense of becoming "special" by doing what most people hadn't the strength of will to do. The hunger was hell, so were the violent exercises which became a daily ritual; but the hell was far outweighed by the reward—the purgation, the shedding of a physical burden, and more important, the shedding of a crippling emotional burden, my conscience. There was a complete shift of emphasis where my conscience was concerned; instead of feeling a burning guilt sensation over almost everything I did, my conscience became concentrated on food and eating, and as long as I abstained from these, my conscience was defeated, and subsided. Its hardly surprising that I clung so vehemently to this panacea which seemed to have miraculously presented itself, a fortress which rendered me impregnable.

To describe the ensuing years as a time when that fortress gradually and imperceptibly became converted into a cage and a prison, would be to employ terminology familiar to anyone with a knowledge of anorexia; nevertheless, it is a very relevant analogy. I'm now 35, and the past 18 years have consisted of increasing awareness, physical pain, wretched depression, isolation, fear of the future, and a struggle to lead anything resembling a normal life. My mind is dominated by contamination and the necessity to escape from it, contamination by food, disease, and human or animal contact. I've become trapped in a futile search for purity and aestheticism, a hopeless attempt to be "special", "refined", on a higher plane. I have a small but loyal circle of friends, whom I value and who have great sensitivity towards my problem; but I spend most of my time "opting out" and alone. I rent a room at the top of a friend's house, where I'm rarely disturbed, and I seek refuge in solitary pursuits, literature, music, and above all, sleep. My dreams are vivid, and permeated by recurrent themes, predatory animals, excrement, food, oranges, eggs, menstruation, sex, pregnancy, cancer, surgery, death, all inextricably connected. I have some contact with my family, with whom my relationship is loving and honest, as they, too, have acquired greater awareness and understanding; but I don't see them very often, partly because of the pain involved for both parties, and partly because independence doesn't come easily or naturally to me therefore I feel it's vital I maintain it. My sister and brother lead settled emotional lives, and both have children, factors which provide my mother with the reassurance that at least the damage for which she holds herself entirely responsible didn't afflict *all* her children.

My view of food and weight has altered considerably over the years, although the underlying phobic fear has remained constant, I suppose. The food itself, which in the early stages was something desirable but forbidden, has gradually changed into an actual source of terror and pollution, and the sight of any food that is imperfect, or worse, putrid, makes me feel suicidal. Every step I take is accompanied by the fear of what food I might encounter, round the next corner or in the room I'm about to enter. I feel guilty with each mouthful I take, especially in public; but I think at long last I've devised a method of eating which, though pathetic, I can maintain, and will at least prevent me from slipping again below the weight I've held for the past year or so, unsatisfactory as that may be. Unlike many anorexics, "bingeing" and vomiting have never been aspects of my illness, nor am I preoccupied with calories, or with cooking which I loathe. The fullest extent of my cooking is the occasional omelette, and I shudder at the mere idea of cooking for other people and plying them with food, an exercise which seems to afford some anorexics great satisfaction. To me, forcing food on others is a cardinal sin. The central items of my diet are cheese and yoghurt. I'm terrified of kitchens and food shops. My two periods of hospital treatment have been physical and mental torture, reducing me to a cabbage, exacerbating my antipathy towards eating, and leaving me with a dread of the medical and psychiatric profession.

My concept of weight is of course, distorted. Thin people arouse in me a fierce jealousy and anguish; overweight people are utterly grotesque, and no sight is more horrendous than that of a pregnant woman. Where my own body is concerned, I don't think I have a warped idea of my appearance, though I may be wrong. I don't see myself as huge when I look in the mirror, I know I'm considerably underweight, unattractively so, but I'm not so thin as to merit the description "skeletal". I'm not addicted to bathroom scales, I weigh myself every few months, and am thoroughly ashamed of the inward relief if I've lost any weight, or the panic if I've gained. I used to derive enormous satisfaction from my protruding ribs; now I still have a desperate need to be thin, but the sight of myself causes me intense panic, I consider myself utterly pathetic, and my inability to face the prospect of a healthy, mature, female body, for which part of me yearns, causes me constant misery and conflict.

Conflict is probably the central and most poignant element of anorexia. Every constructive impulse in me, urging me to participate in life, is counteracted by a stronger destructive impulse, which forces me into withdrawal and isolation. Nowhere is the conflict more fierce than in the sphere of relationships. I long for involvement with people, and sometimes the affection I feel tears me to shreds; but in opposition is the deeply ingrained notion of a cruel world infested with swarms of obnoxious human creatures, from whom I must remain aloof. To associate with them would be to reduce myself to "ordinary" "animal" status. Fortunately I have a job which brings me into contact with many people and enables me to achieve some kind of compromise between involvement and total isolation; I can remain in the background, yet feel the warmth of company. But being with other people is always an enormous strain, and I continually reject opportunities to participate, looking forward all the time to the moment when I'll be alone again.

Where specifically *hetero*sexual relationships are concerned, my conflict is even greater. If I'm honest, what I most long for in life is a close relationship with a man, any hope of achieving this has disappeared, but the wish remains. Despite psychiatrists' insistence on loss of libido in anorexia, I feel very conscious of the strength of sexual feeling within me and my capacity for sexual pleasure, and the fact that this feeling has no gratification is a source of perpetual pain. The majority of men are rather repulsive to me, but there are some whom I find attractive, and this attraction is always accompanied by shame and guilt. Most of the time I feel secure in the knowledge that men don't find me attractive, and won't return any interest I feel; but if a man does show an interest in me, which still happens occasionally, I feel a momentary pleasure, which is immediately obliterated by a sickening sensation of utter depression and humiliation. I used to have some physical contact with men, though never intercourse, and it caused me much distress and degradation. Now I'm too exhausted to even attempt to analyse my sexual fears, let alone overcome them; and the fact that I shall always be alone and never have a family, is just one of the many intolerable aspects of my life.

In theory I suppose I could still, with more determination, fight to improve the worthless quality of my life. During my twenties I did make a supreme effort in this direction, and for a few years attained and held my target weight, and sustained the greater participation this involved. But I couldn't withstand the pressure and the agony, and it was an enormous relief when an attack of glandular fever set me on the downward path again. Now I'm defeated, cynical, sceptical, pessimistic, weary of living, and devoid of motivation and resources. I haven't relinquished altogether the last vestige of hope that change is still possible, but when mere existence consists of struggling to keep my head above a sea of contaminated quicksand, there's no energy or strength left for the ordeal of change.

I now feel able to say something of how I have progressed during the 2½ years since I left hospital. Leaving there with the confidence that I was a complete success it came as a nasty shock when things didn't go smoothly and the old problems began to recur.

I have been back at my target weight for at least six months now. I still have occasional moments of fret and panic—often the result of physical symptoms like indigestion—but I can now enjoy my food without any great sensation of guilt and I drink as and when I feel like it (always my worst problem) without a second thought.

This news is particularly good as I have just passed through one of the potentially most stressful situations, my final exams. I returned to University after leaving hospital and had to repeat two terms beginning in the middle of a year when everyone had already established their friends and I did experience the pains of severe loneliness, but I have battled through and got an honours degree. I am naturally delighted and feel that my decision to persevere has been rewarded.

I have spent the last three summers teaching groups of foreign students and feel confirmed in my early desire to teach. As friends observed I seemed to blossom during these teaching periods and I have now embarked upon a Postgraduate Certificate Course in Education. I am really looking forward to this year and to ultimately getting a job and becoming independent—about time too as I am already 23!

As I inferred, this stage has not been reached without a lot of anguish. My weight dropped dramatically during the first six months after I left hospital and only began to level off when I got a summer job. I am quite sure that this was a direct indicator of the tension I was experiencing.

When I was in hospital my parents presented themselves as "good" and it is true that on the surface (to me as well) they appeared everything that good loving parents should be. But perhaps even this can be overdone. During the last five years my life has been one long struggle to escape the strong but subtle domination of my mother. She has a very strong will and can still influence the lives of my older married sisters. My younger sister really has very little personality of her own and makes no decisions for herself at all. Looking at the situation as objectively as possible, I believe that I have probably got the strongest personality of the sisters and I suppose that it was the need to assert this and prove my own identity that made me challenge my mother's authority.

My father, who has been ill himself for the last two years and has had to retire early as a result, has been most sympathetic and willing to listen and to learn. He has altered a lot during the years and has been a great source of support to all his daughters, especially me. But I feel, and my father would corroborate, that Mum has not learned anything. She is still inflexible and pushes Dad beyond the limits of his physical capacities just as she has always driven me to do more than I am physically, emotionally or intellectually capable of.

The point I am trying to make is that although anorexia may hit one victim it is very much a family problem. I only had a few family sessions during my five months in hospital because my parents lived so far away, and in retrospect I wish we had had many more. My mother has a wonderful skill of being polite, correct and unperturbed to the general observer. She is marvellous at covering uncomfortable feelings and pretending nothing is wrong and tries to ignore tensions which only fester and increase in her frustrated relations. Her niceness has been noted with wonder by neighbours as well as by relations and it is not surprising that I was made to feel guilty for challenging her. It is a tragic situation that "when the younger rises the old must fall" and with the help of the insight I was taught in hospital, I have tried hard to speak and act with Mum as a friend and equal but the relationship rarely lasts more than a week and then I return to my old state of despair and depression, suffer severe inertia and find I can neither fight nor escape the subtle pressures or emotional blackmail exerted upon me.

I realize that I will never change my mother and I look forward to getting a job and my own flat as the real completion of my recovery. But I felt it worthwhile to describe the tip of the iceberg in the hope that it might help other patients.

I have been very lucky in having good friends with whom I have been able to discuss my problems and gain some degree of confidence in my own ability. One of my neighbours particularly encouraged me to return to university and has stood by me in some of the worse times. She is a great morale-booster and always able to look on the optimistic side and my success is really her success too. I still don't see her very often and instead of focussing all my needs on one single mother-substitute, I find myself able to talk to a wide variety of people and this is probably the greatest gift gained in hospital. The ability to express my fears and frustrations has helped me to open out, look beyond myself and understand people better. My willingness to tell my problems has often led others to divulge as well and I hope this has been a help to them.

Confidence in oneself is one of the greatest gaps in an anorexic. Not having developed and experienced life like our "normal" contemporaries we feel odd, misfits from society. Hospitalization obviously saved my life as well as helping me to begin to face it and I am now well enough to be sincerely grateful for that, but the experience makes me wonder whether it is possible to include more preparations for the outer world after one reaches one's adult weight. The month or so seemed a very long time when I was the patient, but in retrospect I feel it might be worth it if it helps to speed up the final process of recovery. The hospital takes us away from the pressures which we couldn't cope with, but they are still there when we are discharged. You have to do a very thorough "job" on the individual patient if she is to be made strong enough to contend with these adverse pressures. The counselling sessions go a long way towards this and were obviously the main lifebuoy to which I have been able to cling. But the world is a very frightening and exacting place and I think from my experience it would have helped to have been forced to face it while still in a protective environment.

The scars I still retain are gradually lessening and I hope that the memories and the experience will now be of use in helping others. I certainly hope that my history will be of encouragement to other patients. My success wasn't as direct and immediate as we hoped but the trend has always been forwards.

It's difficult to pinpoint a precise time when anorexia took over. Unlike most anorexics I never consciously went on a diet. The more I've thought about how it all started the more clearly it seems that patterns of feeling and behaviour established very early on in my childhood led to this particular form of dead-end escape.

I think the first time that compulsive no-eating became incapacitating was when I was 19. I'd recently won two top university scholarships and I was told the world was at my feet. I went to Venice on a two month pre-University course and steadily lost weight. I remember two kinds of feelings as I stepped off the train at Victoria to meet my mother, a pride in my new super slim figure and a sense of relief in the fragility of my body. This sense of fragility had been a sort of protection while I was abroad, protection against homesickness and against the pressures of living alongside boys and girls of my own age and confronting my own sexual feelings and those I aroused in men. I am sure now that the loss of weight and the return to a pre-pubertal asexual bodily state was a subconscious escape from sexuality and my inability to cope with it.

I spent the summer before I went to college at home, steadily losing weight. I'd got myself firmly locked into a compulsive eating pattern which, at a conscious level, was triggered off by a massive fear of indigestion. I dreaded the blown up stomach, the lack of appetite (hunger did at least make you feel alive) and the deep depression all of which were the penalties for eating "too much". I was obsessed by the need to regulate my food to ward off this danger and this led to non-stop calorie counting and, after a few years, to non-stop weighing out of food. The urge to control food supplies in the family also encouraged me to take over more cooking. Cookery had been an absorbing interest ever since I was about eight or nine; it was one spin-off of my constant preoccupation with food.

As a child I was bright, dreamy, highly nervous, unsure of myself and was conscious of a lack of feminine prettiness and charm. (In contrast my elder sister was dainty and ultra-feminine with the confidence of one who was eldest of six.) I longed for popularity and friends and at junior school would have given anything to belong to the charmed circle of girls who were generally approved and accepted.

Behind this lack of poise and self-assertiveness lay the uncertainties, safety and dangers of life at home. I came from a comfortably-off upper middle-class home. My father was a remote figure until I was about 12. A successful lawyer and later a brilliant industrialist, he worked long hours and only intermittently showed much interest in his growing brood. At times, he was frightening, especially when he doled out spankings for some crime. He had a way of typecasting his children: my oldest sister was feminine and pretty, while the third sister was "the practical one", I was the favourite and typecast as sensitive, artistic and intellectual. It was always obvious that he did prefer me and this must have been painful to my brother and sisters and certainly caused resentment on my mother's part.

Dad had some eccentric attitudes to food which must have influenced me, though I don't remember thinking much about it. He had a distaste for obesity which was almost a moral attitude, he was devoted to the ideal of physical fitness and in the war had taken pride in serving as a lean brown "desert rat". As a boy of 19, this "secret" only emerged when I was already anorexic, he had almost died from starvation because he thought he could cure himself of constipation by fasting.

My mother was under some strain. She had very little moral support from my father and never reconciled herself to his absences. She was often pregnant, always busy and her attention was not always easy to come by. Yet we each craved it and competed for it. Neither of my parents had many friends and I think they both found intimacy with their children and with others a difficult thing to achieve.

From the pressures of school and home my greatest escape and joy was reading. However I did gradually discover ways in which I could gain some acceptance at school. My schoolwork earned praise from the teachers. I discovered that my superior wit and articulacy could earn some respect and even some friends among my classmates. It was by being "interesting" and extraordinary that I could fight my way to an identity of my own. All this of course was very strenuous and home was a precious sanctuary from the outside world. I suffered from terrible homesickness if ever I went away. At 13 I remember a disastrous visit to a French penfriend when I was so miserable that I stopped eating and was fed on rice pudding.

At secondary school my lack of sexual experience and my lack of interest in make up and the pop scene cut me off from my classmates. I tried to make up for these eccentricities by my intellectual achievements and in the end I was quite successful. I suppose I was more inclined to daydream about food and recipes than any of my classmates. Yet I did at times experience strong sexual feelings, when I listened to music, read a romantic novel or developed a passionate crush on some unattainable male.

At college, I was thin and weak and devoted my terms mainly to work, the holidays I spent mainly at home reclining and recuperating. As soon as any boy showed the slightest physical interest I broke it off. The worst thing was my total lack of poise. Ordinary social contacts would be terrifying as my fragile hold on myself became threatened by the personality of the other. The usual escape route via intellectual prowess became blocked, it wasn't so easy to shine in Oxbridge as in a grammar school and my poor health became an increasing liability.

I was hospitalized after I'd taken my (not very distinguished) degree. I was kept in bed, doped silly with Largactil and urged to eat anything and everything. In the end I discharged myself and promptly lost all the weight I'd gained. Five anorexic years later, in desperation, I asked to be admitted to another hospital. The combination of a carefully regulated diet, bedrest plus psychotherapy made that stay a turning point, and I left hospital with more conviction that I had *some* worth as a person than I'd felt before. The only part of the treatment which I felt then and now was of value only to my therapists was the "family therapy". This must have given staff insight into my case but it aroused a lot of pain and guilt in my parents—feelings which were never worked through properly in the three sessions allotted to this therapy.

Since leaving hospital there have been dispiriting setbacks. But over these five years, I have changed and grown freer than I could have dared hope.

One big mistake was to return to my university town where I'd been living before going into hospital. In the dangerous security of my tiny circle of friends and the close tie to my charismatic Director of Studies I had little chance of finding myself. It does seem to be of real importance that there is a stimulating and fresh environment to live in once hospital treatment is completed. I take responsibility for the decision to go back to my old haunts, but I still wish my scrupulously non-directive therapist had said "don't go back".

My first big break was coming to London, to a totally new world, my first proper job and my first vexed unsatisfying off-on relationship with a man. It was the first time I had ever had *any* sexual relationship.

Just before the move, my father died after a car crash. I can't properly analyse my feelings at that time. I remember flying down from Scotland to London with the general feeling that on the one hand I wouldn't care if the plane crashed and on the other hand a sense of new purpose, a greater freedom.

I can single out three things which have helped me: holding down a job which

I could do competently, learning the Alexander technique and gaining a new sense of poise and pride in my body and a way of dealing with some of the tensions I carried around, asking and getting the help of the psychiatric social worker I'd met in the hospital. She and I worked hard. I got back my pounds and my periods. I felt more alive, sexy and outgoing. I had my first affair. Marvellously, I found myself valued as much, if not more, for my physical attractions as for my intellect and sensitivity.

There was a sad unsettled period after the affair ended. The self-destructive drive which led to anorexia was not buried, only temporarily in abeyance. I lost weight again. Now I'm struggling once again to regain and hold onto the lost pounds. After so many years the eating habits which propel me back to the sleep-walking half-life I dread are very firmly ingrained. But I've proved in the past I can win out. I have a different idea of who I am. I can risk more. If I have done all I can to ensure that I can live life fully and intensely then in a way the rest doesn't matter. I can be at peace with myself.

Appendix 1(a)
Average body weights at different ages and heights
(From Kemsley, W. F. F. (1953/54) *Ann. Eugen. London*, **16**, 316–334)

Table A. Graduated mean weights (lb.) at each age and height—males

Age	Height (in)														
	60	61	62	63	64	65	66	67	68	69	70	71	72	73	74
15	96	101	105	109	113	117	122	126	130	134	138	143	147	151	155
16	99	104	108	112	116	120	124	128	132	136	140	145	149	153	157
17	103	107	111	115	119	123	127	131	135	139	143	147	151	155	159
18	106	110	113	117	121	125	129	133	137	141	145	148	152	156	160
19	109	112	116	120	124	128	132	135	139	143	147	150	154	158	162
20	111	115	119	122	126	130	134	137	141	145	148	152	156	159	163
21	114	117	121	124	128	132	135	139	142	146	150	153	157	160	164
22	115	119	122	126	130	133	137	140	144	148	151	155	158	162	166
23	116	120	124	127	131	134	138	142	145	149	152	156	160	163	167
24	117	121	124	128	132	135	139	142	146	150	153	157	160	164	168
27	118	121	125	129	132	136	140	144	147	151	155	158	162	166	169
32	120	123	127	131	134	138	142	146	149	153	157	160	164	168	172
37	121	124	128	132	136	139	143	147	150	154	158	162	165	169	173
42	121	125	128	132	136	140	143	147	150	154	158	162	165	169	173
47	122	125	129	133	136	140	144	148	151	155	159	162	166	170	174
52	122	126	130	134	137	141	145	148	152	156	159	163	167	170	174
57	123	127	131	134	138	142	146	149	153	157	160	164	167	171	175
62	124	128	132	135	139	143	146	150	154	158	161	165	168	172	176
67	125	129	133	136	140	144	147	151	155	158	162	166	170	173	177

Table B. Graduated mean weights (lb) at each age and height—females

Age	Height (in)														
	56	57	58	59	60	61	62	63	64	65	66	67	68	69	70
15	84	88	92	96	100	104	108	112	115	119	123	127	131	135	139
16	90	93	97	100	104	107	111	114	118	121	125	128	132	135	139
17	94	97	101	104	107	110	113	117	120	123	126	129	133	136	139
18	96	99	102	105	109	112	115	118	121	125	128	131	134	137	141
19	97	100	103	106	110	113	116	119	122	126	129	132	135	138	142
20	98	101	104	107	110	114	117	120	123	126	130	133	136	139	142
21	98	101	104	108	111	114	117	120	123	127	130	133	136	139	143
22	98	102	105	108	111	114	118	121	124	127	130	134	137	140	143
23	98	102	105	108	111	114	118	121	124	127	130	134	137	140	143
24	99	102	106	109	112	115	118	121	124	127	130	133	136	140	143
27	100	103	106	109	112	116	119	122	125	128	131	134	137	140	144
32	103	106	109	112	115	118	121	124	127	130	133	136	139	142	145
37	106	109	112	115	118	121	124	127	130	133	136	139	142	145	148
42	111	114	117	120	123	126	129	132	134	137	140	143	146	149	152
47	115	118	120	123	126	129	132	135	138	141	144	146	149	152	155
52	117	120	123	126	128	131	134	137	140	142	145	148	151	154	156
57	117	120	123	126	129	131	134	137	140	143	145	148	151	154	157
62	116	119	122	124	127	130	133	136	138	141	144	147	150	152	155
67	113	116	119	122	124	127	130	133	136	138	141	144	147	150	152

Appendix 1(b)
Units of weight conversion tables

lb	stone	lb	kg	lb	stone	lb	kg
56	4	0	25·4	116	8	4	52·6
57	4	1	25·9	117	8	5	53·1
58	4	2	26·3	118	8	6	53·5
59	4	3	26·8	119	8	7	54·0
60	4	4	27·2	120	8	8	54·4
61	4	5	27·7	121	8	9	54·9
62	4	6	28·1	122	8	10	55·3
63	4	7	28·6	123	8	11	55·8
64	4	8	29·0	124	8	12	56·3
65	4	9	29·5	125	8	13	56·7
66	4	10	29·9	126	9	0	57·2
67	4	11	30·4	127	9	1	57·6
68	4	12	30·8	128	9	2	58·1
69	4	13	31·3	129	9	3	58·5
70	5	0	31·8	130	9	4	59·0
71	5	1	32·2	131	9	5	59·4
72	5	2	32·7	132	9	6	59·9
73	5	3	33·1	133	9	7	60·3
74	5	4	33·6	134	9	8	60·8
75	5	5	34·0	135	9	9	61·2
76	5	6	34·5	136	9	10	61·7
77	5	7	34·9	137	9	11	62·1
78	5	8	35·4	138	9	12	62·6
79	5	9	35·8	139	9	13	63·1
80	5	10	36·3	140	10	0	63·5
81	5	11	36·7	141	10	1	64·0
82	5	12	37·2	142	10	2	64·4
83	5	13	37·7	143	10	3	64·9
84	6	0	38·1	144	10	4	65·3
85	6	1	38·6	145	10	5	65·8
86	6	2	39·0	146	10	6	66·2
87	6	3	39·5	147	10	7	66·7
88	6	4	39·9	148	10	8	67·1
89	6	5	40·4	149	10	9	67·6
90	6	6	40·8	150	10	10	68·0
91	6	7	41·3	151	10	11	68·5
92	6	8	41·7	152	10	12	69·0
93	6	9	42·2	153	10	13	69·4
94	6	10	42·6	154	11	0	69·9
95	6	11	43·1	155	11	1	70·3
96	6	12	43·6	156	11	2	70·8
97	6	13	44·0	157	11	3	71·2
98	7	0	44·5	158	11	4	71·7
99	7	1	44·9	159	11	5	72·1
100	7	2	45·4	160	11	6	72·6
101	7	3	45·8	161	11	7	73·0
102	7	4	46·3	162	11	8	73·5
103	7	5	46·7	163	11	9	73·9
104	7	6	47·2	164	11	10	74·4
105	7	7	47·6	165	11	11	74·8
106	7	8	48·1	166	11	12	75·3
107	7	9	48·5	167	11	13	75·8
108	7	10	49·0	168	12	0	76·2
109	7	11	49·4	169	12	1	76·7
110	7	12	49·9	170	12	2	77·1
111	7	13	50·4	171	12	3	77·6
112	8	0	50·8	172	12	4	78·0
113	8	1	51·3	173	12	5	78·5
114	8	2	51·7	174	12	6	78·9
115	8	3	52·2	175	12	7	79·4

Appendix II

The following is a chronological list of the principal scientific and review publications in the area of anorexia nervosa over the last 30 years of the author and his team. It is included here in case some readers wish to explore such exact evidence as there is for some of the assertions in this book.

Crisp, A. H. and Roberts, F. J. (1962). A case of anorexia nervosa in a male. *Postgrad. Med. J.* **38**, 350-353.

Crisp, A. H. (1965). Clinical and therapeutic aspects of anorexia nervosa: A study of 30 cases. *J. Psychosom. Res.* **9**, 67-78.

—— (1965) Some aspects of the evolution, presentation and follow-up of anorexia nervosa. *Proc. Roy. Soc. Med.* **58**, 814-820.

——, Ellis, J. and Lowy, C. (1967). Insulin response to a rapid intravenous injection of dextrose in patients with anorexia nervosa and obesity. *Postgrad. Med. J.* **43**, 97-102.

—— (1967). The possible significance of some behavioural correlates of weight and carbohydrate intake. *J. Psychosom. Res.* **11**, 117-131.

—— and Stonehill, E. (1967). Hypercarotenaemia as a symptom of weight phobia. *Postgrad. Med. J.* **43**, 721-725.

Blendis, L. M. and Crisp, A. H. (1968). Serum cholesterol levels in anorexia nervosa. *Postgrad. Med. J.* **44**, 327-330.

Crisp, A. H., Fenton, G. W. and Scotton, L. (1968). A controlled study of the EEG in anorexia nervosa. *Brit. J. Psychiat.* **114**, 1149-1160.

——, Blendis, L. M. and Pawan, G. L. S. (1968). Aspects of fat metabolism in anorexia nervosa. *Metabolism, Clinical and Experimental* **17**, 1109-1118.

—— (1969). Psychological aspects of breast-feeding with particular reference to anorexia nervosa. *Brit. J. Med. Psychol.* **42**, 119-132.

—— (1969). Some skeletal measurements in patients with primary anorexia nervosa. *J. Psychosom. Res.* **13**, 125-142.

—— (1970). Premorbid factors in adult disorders of weight, with particular reference to primary anorexia nervosa (weight phobia). A literature review. *J. Psychosom. Res.* **14**, 1-22.

—— (1970). Reported birth weights and growth rates in a group of patients with primary anorexia nervosa (weight phobia). *J. Psychosom. Res.* **14**, 23-50.

——(1970). Anorexia nervosa 'feeding disorder', 'nervous malnutrition' or 'weight phobia'. *World Review of Nutrition and Dietetics* **12**, 452-504.

—— and Stonehill, E. (1971). Relation between aspects of nutritional disturbance and menstrual activity in primary anorexia nervosa. *Brit. Med.* **3**, 149-151.

Crisp, A. H. and Toms, D. A. (1972). Primary anorexia nervosa or weight phobia in the male. Report on 13 cases. *Brit. Med. J.* **1**, 334-338.

—— and Fransella, F. (1972). Conceptual changes during recovery from anorexia nervosa. *Brit. J. Med. Psychol.* **45**, 395-405.

——, MacKinnon, P. C. B., Chen, C. N. and Corker, C. S. (1973). Observations of gonadotrophic and ovarian hormone activity during recovery from anorexia nervosa. *Postgrad. Med. J.* **49**, 584-590.

—— and Kalucy, R. S. (1973). The effect of leucotomy in intractable adolescent weight phobia (primary anorexia nervosa). *Postgrad. Med. J.* **49**,883-893.

——, Harding, B. and McGuiness, B. (1974). Anorexia nervosa: Psychoneurotic characteristics of parents - Relationship to prognosis. A quantitative study. *J. Psychosom. Res.* **18**, 167-173.

—— and Kalucy, R. S. (1974). Aspects of the perceptual disorder in anorexia nervosa. *Brit. J. Med. Psychol.* **47**, 349-361.

Palmer, R. L., Crisp, A. H., MacKinnon, P. C. B., Franklin, M., Bonnar, J. and Wheeler, M. (1975). Pituitary sensitivity to 50 g LH/FSH-RH in subjects with anorexia nervosa in acute and recovery stages. *Brit. Med. J.* **1**, 179-182.

Lacey, J. H., Crisp, A. H., Kalucy, R. S., Hartman, M. K. and Chen, C. N. (1975). Weight gain and the sleeping EEG. A study of 10 patients with anorexia nervosa. *Brit. Med. J.* **4**, 556-559.

Crisp, A. H., Palmer, R. L. and Kalucy, R. S. (1976). How common is anorexia nervosa? A prevalence study. *Brit. J. Psychiat.* **128**, 549-554.

Kalucy, R. S., Crisp, A. H., Chard, T., McNeilly, A., Chen, C. N. and Lacey, J. H. (1976). Nocturnal hormonal profiles in massive obesity, anorexia nervosa and normal females. *J. Psychosom. Res.* **20**, 595-604.

Lacey, J. H., Stanley, P. A., Crutchfield, M. and Crisp, A. H. (1977). Sucrose sensitivity in anorexia nervosa. *J. Psychosom. Res.* **21**, 17-21.

Stordy, B. J., Marks, V., Kalucy, R. S. and Crisp, A. H. (1977). Weight gain, thermic effect of glucose and resting metabolic rate during recovery from anorexia nervosa. *Am. J. Clin. Nutr.* **30**, 138-146.

Stonehill, E. and Crisp, A. H. (1977). Psychoneurotic characteristics of patients with anorexia nervosa before and after treatment and at follow-up 4-7 years later. *J. Psychosom. Res.* **21**, 187-193.

Hurst, P. S., Lacey, J. H. and Crisp, A. H. (1977). Teeth, vomiting and diet: A study of the dental characteristics of 17 anorexia nervosa patients. *Postgrad. Med. J.* **53**, 298-305.

Crisp, A. H. (1977). Some psychobiological aspects of adolescent growth and their relevance for the fat/thin syndrome (anorexia nervosa). *Int. J. Obesity* **1**, 231-238.

——, Kalucy, R. S., Lacey, J. H. and Harding, B. (1977). The long-term prognosis in anorexia nervosa: Some factors predictive of outcome. *Anorexia Nervosa*, Ed. Vigersky, R.A., Raven Press, New York. pp 55-65.

—— (1977). Diagnosis and outcome of anorexia nervosa: The St. George's view. *Proc. Roy. Soc. Med.* **70**, 464-470.

Crisp, A. H. (1977). The differential diagnosis of anorexia nervosa. *Proc. Roy. Soc. Med.* **70**, 686-694.

Pillay, M. and Crisp, A. H. (1977). Some psychological characteristics of patients with anorexia nervosa whose weight has been newly restored. *Brit. J. Med. Psychol.* **50**, 375-380.

Kalucy, R. S., Crisp, A. H. and Harding, B. (1977). A study of 56 families with anorexia nervosa. *Brit. J. Med. Psychol.* **50**, 381-395.

Crisp, A. H. (1978). Some aspects of the relationship between body weight and sexual behaviour with particular reference to massive obesity and anorexia nervosa. *Int. J. Obesity* **2**, 17-32.

Armstrong-Esther, C. A., Lacey, J. H., Crisp, A. H. and Bryant, T. N. (1978). An investigation of the immune response of patients suffering from anorexia nervosa. *Postgrad. Med. J.* **54**, 395-399.

Crisp, A. H. (1978). Disturbances of neurotransmitter metabolism in anorexia nervosa. *Proc. Nutr. Soc.* **37**, 151-159.

Hsu, L. K. G., Crisp, A. H. and Harding, B. (1979). Outcome of anorexia nervosa. *Lancet* **i**, 62-65.

Lacey, J. H., Crisp, A. H., Hart, G. and Kirkwood, B. A. (1979). Weight and skeletal maturation - a study of radiological and chronological age in an anorexia nervosa population. *Postgrad. Med. J.* **55**, 381-385.

Crisp, A. H., Hsu, L. K. G. and Stonehill, E. (1979). Personality, body weight and ultimate outcome in anorexia nervosa. *J. Clin. Psychiat.* **40**, 332-335.

Ben-Tovim, D. I., Whitehead, J. and Crisp, A. H. (1979). A controlled study of the perception of body width in anorexia nervosa. *J. Psychosom. Res.* **23**, 267-272.

Ben-Tovim, D. I., Marilov, V. and Crisp, A. H. (1979). Personality and mental state (PSE) within anorexia nervosa. *J. Psychosom. Res.* **23**, 321-325.

Crisp, A. H., Hsu, L. K. G., Harding, B. and Hartshorn, J. (1980). Clinical features of anorexia nervosa. A study of a consecutive series of 102 female patients. *J. Psychosom. Res.* **24**, 179-191.

———, Hsu, L. K. G. and Harding, B. (1980). The starving hoarder and voracious spender: Stealing in anorexia nervosa. *J. Psychosom. Res.* **24**, 225-231.

Hsu, L. K. G., Meltzer, E. and Crisp, A. H. (1981). Schizophrenia and anorexia nervosa. *J. Nerv. Ment. Dis.* **169**, 5, 273-276.

Crisp, A.H. (1981). Anorexia nervosa at normal body weight! - The abnormal normal weight control syndrome. *Int. J. Psychiatry in Medicine* **11**, (3), 203-233.

———, Hsu, L. K. G., Chen, C. N. and Wheeler, M. (1982). Reproductive hormone profiles in male anorexia nervosa before, during and after restoration of body weight to normal. A study of 12 patients. *Int. J. Eating Disorders* **1**, (3), 3-9.

——— and Burns, T. (1983). The clinical presentation of anorexia nervosa in males. *Int. J. Eating Disorders* **2**, No. 4, 5-10.

——— (1983). Anorexia Nervosa. (Regular review) *Brit. Med. J.* **287**, 855-858.

——— (1983). Anorexia nervosa: Getting the 'heat' out of the system. *Psychiatric Annals* **13**, 936-952.

Crisp, A. H. (1984). Treatment of anorexia nervosa: What can be the role of psychopharmacological agents? *The Psychobiology of Anorexia Nervosa*, Eds. Pirke, K.M. and Ploog, D., Springer-Verlag, Heidelberg. pp 148-160.

Burns, T. and Crisp, A. H. (1984). Outcome of anorexia nervosa in males. *Brit. J. Psychiat.* **145**, 319-325.

Crisp, A. H. (1985). Gastrointestinal disturbance in anorexia nervosa. *Postgrad. Med. J.* **61**, 3-5.

Ben-Tovim, D. I. and Crisp, A.H. (1984). The reliability of estimates of body width and their relationship to current measured body size among anorexic and normal subjects. *Psychol. Med.* **14**, 843-846.

Crisp, A. H., Hall, A. and Holland, A. J. (1985). Nature and nurture in anorexia nervosa: A study of 34 pairs of twins, one pair of triplets and an adoptive family. *Int. J. Eating Disorders* **4**, 5-27.

—— (1985). Regulation of the self in adolescence with particular reference to anorexia nervosa. *Transactions of the Medical Society of London* **100**, 67-74.

——, Norton, K. R. W., Jurczak, S., Bowyer, C. and Duncan, S. (1985). A treatment approach to anorexia nervosa - 25 years on. *J. Psychiat. Res.* **19**, 393-404.

Gowers, S., Kadambari, S. R. and Crisp, A. H. (1985). Family structure and birth order of patients with anorexia nervosa. *J. Psychiat. Res.* **19**, 247-251.

Abou-Saleh, M. T., Oleesky, D. A. and Crisp, A. H. (1985). Dexamethasone suppression and energy balance: A study of anorexic patients. *J. Psychiat. Res.* **19**, 203-206.

Crisp, A. H. (1985). Arousal, physical activity, and energy balance in eating and body weight and shape disorders. *Int. J. Eating Disorders* **4**, 627-649.

Abou-Saleh, M. T., Oleesky, D., Crisp, A. H. and Lacey, J. H. (1986). Dexamethasone suppression and energy balance in eating disorders. *Acta Psychiat. Scand.* **73**, 242-251.

Crisp, A. H., Burns, T. and Bhat, A. V. (1986). Primary anorexia nervosa in the male and female: A comparison of clinical features and prognosis. *Brit. J. Med. Psychol.* **59**, 123-132.

——, Matthews, B., Norton, K. R. W. and Oakey, M. (1986). Weight-related attitudes and behaviour in anorexics, recovered anorexics and normals. *Int. J. Eating Disorders* **5**, 789-798.

——, Mayer, C. N. and Bhat, A. V. (1986). Patterns of weight gain in a group of patients treated for anorexia nervosa. *Int. J. Eating Disorders* **5**, (6), 1007-1024.

—— (1986). The integration of 'self-help' and 'help' in the prevention of anorexia nervosa. *British Review of Bulimia and Anorexia Nervosa* **1**, 27-39.

——, Lacey, J. H. and Crutchfield, M. (1987). Clomipramine and 'drive' in people with anorexia nervosa: An in-patient study. *Brit. J. Psychiat.* **150**, 355-358.

Hall, A. and Crisp, A. H. (1987). Brief psychotherapy in the treatment of anorexia nervosa. Outcome at one year. *Brit. J. Psychiat.* **151**, 186-191.

Crisp, A. H. (1988). Some possible approaches to prevention of eating and body weight/shape disorders, with particular reference to anorexia nervosa. *Int. J. Eating Disorders* 7, 1-17.

———, Gowers, S., Matthews, B., Oakey, M. Crutchfield, M. and O'Neill, M. (1988). Communicating with the anorectic patient: Engaging with the body or mind? *Eating Disorders in Adolescents and Young Adults*, Eds. Hardoff, D. and Chigier, E., Freund Publishing, London. pp 89-97.

Heavey, A., Parker, Y., Bhat, A. V., Crisp, A. H. and Gowers, S. G. (1989). Anorexia nervosa and marriage. *Int. J. Eating Disorders* 8, 275-284.

Crisp, A. H., Joughin, N., Halek, C. and Bowyer, C. (1989). *Anorexia Nervosa and the Wish to Change*: Selfhelp and Discovery, the Thirty Steps. Department of Mental Health Sciences, St. George's Hospital Medical School, London.

Gowers, S. G. and Crisp, A. H. (1990). Anorexia nervosa in an 80-year-old woman. *Brit. J. Psychiat.* 157, 754-757.

Gowers, S. G., Crisp, A. H., Joughin, N. and Bhat, A. (1991). Premenarchal anorexia nervosa. *J. Child Psychol. Psychiat.* 32, (3), 515-524.

Crisp, A. H., Norton, K., Gowers, S., Halek, C., Bowyer, C., Yeldham, D., Levett, G., and Bhat, A. (1991). A controlled study of the effect of therapies aimed at adolescent and family psychopathology in anorexia nervosa. *Brit. J. Psychiat.* 159, 325-333.

Joughin, N. A., Crisp, A. H., Gowers, S. G. and Bhat, A. V. (1991). The clinical features of late onset anorexia nervosa. *Postgrad. Med. J.* 67, 973-977.

Crisp, A. H., Callender, J. S., Halek, C. and Hsu, L. K. G. (1992). Long-term mortality in anorexia nervosa. A 20-year follow-up of the St. George's and Aberdeen cohorts. *Brit. J. Psychiat.* 161, 104-107.

Joughin, N., Varsou, E., Gowers, S. and Crisp, A. H. (1992). Relative tallness in anorexia nervosa. *Int. J. Eating Disorders* 12, 193-207.

———, Crisp, A. H., Halek, C. and Humphrey, H. (1992). Religious belief and anorexia nervosa. *Int. J. Eating Disorders* 12, 197-406.

Gowers, S., Norton, K., Halek, C. and Crisp, A. H. (1994). Outcome of outpatient psychotherapy in a random allocation treatment study of anorexia nervosa. *Int. J. Eating Disorders* 15, 165-177.

Crisp, A. H. and McClelland, L. (1994). *Anorexia Nervosa: The "St George's" Approach*. Division of Psychological Medicine, Dept. of Mental Health Sciences, St George's Hospital Medical School, London.

Hindler, C. G., Crisp, A. H., McGuigan, S. and Joughin, N. (1994). Anorexia nervosa: change over time in age of onset, presentation and duration of illness. *Psychol. Med.* 24, 719-729.

Index

Lightning Source UK Ltd.
Milton Keynes UK
04 October 2010

160746UK00011B/16/P